What Once Was Hidden

Laurie Powers

ISBN 978-1-0980-0248-0 (paperback)
ISBN 978-1-0980-0249-7 (digital)

Copyright © 2019 by Laurie Powers

All rights reserved. No part of this publication may be reproduced, distributed, or transmitted in any form or by any means, including photocopying, recording, or other electronic or mechanical methods without the prior written permission of the publisher. For permission requests, solicit the publisher via the address below.

Christian Faith Publishing, Inc.
832 Park Avenue
Meadville, PA 16335
www.christianfaithpublishing.com

Printed in the United States of America

To my circle of prayer warriors who…
refuse to let me battle alone,
stand in the gap when I've laid down my sword,
and remind me often that I have purpose because of Jesus.

Introduction

As a photographer, I have become keenly aware of light. The angle or the softness of light can change the whole feel of an image. It's one of the most important aspects of well-done photography.

I am also a student of *thee* Light. Jesus said, "I am the Light of the world. Whoever follows me will never walk in darkness, but will have the light of life." John 8:12

This book is a compilation of my journals over several years. Each of these stories is something personal to me, but when I held them up to the light of Jesus and let him illuminate his truth on them, they became moments on earth kissed by heaven.

They have become *my* story colliding with *his* story. My prayer is that you will find something of *your* story in these pages.

Enjoy!

A Flat-Tire Blessing

A flat tire. God's answer to my prayer asking how I could bless someone today. No, I didn't stop to help someone. It was *me* who got the flat tire as I was pulling into church.

I called AAA for roadside assistance. Within ten minutes, I was face-to-face with Wayne, an African-American man with short dreads. He hopped out of his vehicle and, after saying hello, went to a cooler on the back of his truck and pulled out a bottle of water, gave it to me, and said, "This is for you."

"*What*? I am the one who just stepped out of an air-conditioned church and you are giving *me* a cool drink of water?" It was such a sweet, random act of kindness.

As he changed out my tire and put on my spare, my mind went back to my question of the morning. Is *this* who you want me to bless, Lord? Of course it was! I knew in an instant that there were two things I wanted to share with Wayne.

As he finished up the task at hand, I said to him, "Wayne, I have two things I want to share with you."

He looked at me like he wasn't sure where this was going.

I said, "Obviously, I'm here at church and this morning I asked God who he wanted me to bless and here you are."

He said, "Everything happens for a reason."

I said, "Yes, it does." I reached into my wallet and pulled out $20 and said, "I would like you to take this and have lunch on me today."

He shook his head in disbelief and said, "Are you kidding me?"

I said, "You know, we all have our stuff that we deal with, and I just want to tell you that God really loves you."

He said, "Yes, we do. I love him too, and I thank you for your kindness."

I'm glad I got a flat tire. It immobilized me to dependency on the help of Wayne. And it mobilized me to look a stranger in the eye and say, "God really loves you."

Lord, I pray that each random act of kindness will cause ripple effects in our lives as we seek to be obedient. I pray that Wayne walked away with a renewal of hope in you and connected to your love in ways I may never know this side of heaven.

A Rare Beauty

In the movie *First Knight*, there is a scene where the king's stableman, Peter, is standing with King Arthur and watching Guinevere test a beautiful mare horse that is to be given to her as a wedding gift from the king. As she trollops around the courtyard, Peter says to the king, "She's a rare beauty, sire." There is a pause as you see the pride on King Arthur's face at the compliment, believing Peter is talking about the horse. He then says, "And so is the mare."

A rare beauty. Has anyone ever called you that? Have *you* ever believed that about yourself? God speaks of you in these terms. He calls us his "treasured possession" in Malachi 3:17. He says he "takes great delight in us" in Zephaniah 3:17.

Ephesians 1:4 says, "Long before he laid down earth's foundations, he had US in mind, had settled on *us* as the focus of his love." You and I are the greatest objects of God's affection!

I believe that many of us, if not all of us, have allowed a repeated message to consume us that asks questions more like this...

Does God want me?
Does God notice me?
Does He really think I am a worthy treasure?
Do I deserve his affection and pursuit?

Asking these kinds of questions reminds me of a dinner show I attended at Disney World called King Henry's Feast. Each guest was ushered in to long tables that spoked out from a center stage. The event began with a king stepping on stage. From the guests, he would pull up one woman after another and ask her if she wanted to be his queen. I watched from my table with a yearning just to be noticed, to feel worthy enough to be brought up on stage. And there I sat, feeling unlovely and unnoticed.

This is so far from the reality of our Creator. We have been more than noticed! He has pursued us and loved us from the beginning of time. He wanted to be with us so passionately, that he came down off the stage of heaven, took on the form of a man, and extended his hands upon a cross so he could take our hand and invite us to a great wedding feast as his bride!

The reality is, most of us live our lives missing the fact that we have stolen the very heart of God. In the Song of Solomon, we read, "You have stolen my heart, my bride; you have stolen my heart."

Can you stop for a minute, go to a mirror, look at yourself, and say the words, "The truest thing about me is what God says about me," and then seek his word for truth?

> He loves you.
> He adores you.
> He wants you.
> He sees you.

Your Creator has placed a passionate longing in your heart that is meant to lead you to him and him alone. He is the *only* Person who can satisfy the ache of the human heart.

And here is where the rub often comes in. God loves us so radically that he will go to whatever means are necessary to woo us to himself. This is often called the refiner's fire.

Do you know that a metallurgist (a scientist who separates metals from their ores to prepare them for their use) will take the greatest care with precious metals? A good refiner will never leave the crucible (the heat-resistant container for melting), just like Malachi 3:3 indicates, "he will sit down" by the fire and watch it so it will not become even one degree too hot and possibly harm the metal. He subjects the metal to a blazing fire to release the dross, the scum, and waste so that what remains is the pure metal. And he knows the proper time to extinguish the fire because he will actually see his face reflected on the surface of the pure metal.

WHAT ONCE WAS HIDDEN

Our Creator does the same thing with us. He sees the rare and precious beauty we are, often when we cannot, and he does what a good refiner will do and takes us through a refining process.

The next time you feel like you have no value? When you give that over to God, the scum of the metal is removed.

When you believe any truth other than God's truth? *Drip, drip*—the dross being removed when you turn back to truth.

When your coworker or friend stabs you in the back and you refuse to gossip about them? *Drip, drip, drip.*

The list goes on. But the refiner stays put.

And every time we allow him to refine us, we move one step closer to being a reflection of him.

You. Are. A. Rare. Beauty.

A Deliberate Walk into Darkness

Have you ever had the experience of standing at the mouth of a cave where light and dark meet? A tour guide and a group of tourists all stepped into the complete and utter darkness without reservation and it has always led me to two thoughts: either we were a very trusting group of people or we were all very gullible.

Think about this with me. Not *one* person, other than the guide, who was a complete stranger, had any ability to light up the cave once we were immersed in total darkness. I'm talking about the kind of darkness that you literally could not see your hand right in front of your face. My overactive imagination began to wonder, "What if the real guide was knocked out by some psycho who wanted to play a cruel joke on us, taking us deep into the bowels of the cave, and then leaving us there with no way out of the darkness?" We had only one person who could lead us to light again.

And isn't that true of Jesus? He is the only One capable of lighting our path out of spiritual darkness.

Psalm 119:105 says, "Your Word is a lamp to my feet and a light for my path."

John 3:19 says, "This is the verdict: Light (Jesus) has come into the world, but people loved darkness instead of light."

When Jesus calls us into relationship with him, he plucks us out of our darkness. He shines a light for us on the path back to light. He is called the Light of the World. And what is so promising is that he doesn't just get us out of our darkness, he transforms us when we step into the Light.

John 12:35–36 says, "Then Jesus told them… The man who walks in the dark does not know where he is going. Put your trust in the light while you have it, *so that* you may *become* sons of light."

It's like he says, "I'm going to give each of you your own personal spiritual flashlight and I am going to offer the never-ending source of power to illuminate your way. Do not be afraid. I know the way out of darkness. Just follow me. I *am* the Light."

A Darkness That Blinds

The course has been laid before us,
The Divine has us each in his hand
So much to see, so much to do
Yet, a plethora of distractive demands.

We traverse down the cobblestone road
And stand before a dead-end door.
Shattered and confused, we retreat,
We had hoped for something much more.

Our vision grows dim as we shift from the Light
That once was our hope and our guide,
Is now covered in fog and the cobwebs of life,
As we run, as we turn, as we hide.

I complacently sit down in the recesses
Of darkness, dripping moisture of fear.
Where do I turn? Where do I go?
How can I know that you're near?

I hear the enemy's laughter
Reveling in my plight.
"No more! No more!" I say.
Give me the will to fight!

There *must* be more! So much more I know
Give me the courage to get up and go!
I turn from the cold and the darkness of night
It's you once again! My warmth and my Light!

A Tomb of Sweetness

I love hummingbirds. They fascinate me. Did you know that they have great memories? They will migrate hundreds and hundreds of miles and return in the summer, stopping at the same feeders all the way back to their final destination. I know this is true because I have had hummingbirds flitting outside my kitchen window where my feeder hangs *before* I put it up. We have three that return every year.

One of the problems with a hummingbird feeder is the attraction of ants. They sense that sweet, sugary smell and before long, they are trailing to the source.

Then, they work hard at finding a way to immerse themselves into the sweetness.

Once they find a way inside the feeder, they bask in it, doing backstrokes of delight.

Before they know it, they are drowning in all that sweetness and are entrapped in it.

What once felt like hitting the jackpot has now become their tomb of death.

And there they are, embalmed in sugar water for all the world to see, but the other ants keep coming, looking for the same sweet promise and ignoring the floating colony of the other ants.

One evening, as my husband and I sat eating dinner, he looked out at the feeder loaded with ants floating and he said, "That's such a picture of sin." He was so right.

We are so like those ants when it comes to sin, aren't we?

We seek its perceived promise of sweetness.

We bask in it and before we know it, we are trapped.

We often ignore the impact it has on others, thinking that somehow we can taste the sweetness, but we know how to control its impact on us.

And before we know it, it leads to spiritual death.

> "There is a way that appears to be right, but
> in the end it leads to death" (Prov. 14:12)

A Mighty Roar

Iguazu Falls in South America are the largest falls in the world. Prior to visiting them, I had only seen Niagara Falls and those amazed me. One of the coolest things about Iguazu Falls is the walkway that takes you right to the base of the falls. As you head down the walkway, you can hear this distant roar of the falls that increases as you get closer. But it's down at the base where you feel its incredible power. The roar of the falls is so loud you can barely hear what others are saying. You feel, hear, and see the power, and it sweeps you away in its majestic display.

I can still see my friend standing in front of the falls and saying, "This reminds me so much of God's love. It's powerful and it's a never-ending source."

As I thought about that, I realized that even this visual fell short of the strength and power of God's holiness, his perfect love, and his multifaceted Being that displays his power *and* his gentleness.

Psalm 29 is a great description of this.

> "The voice of the Lord is over the waters. The voice of the Lord is powerful; the voice of the Lord is majestic. The voice of the Lord breaks the cedars; the Lord breaks into pieces the cedar of Lebanon…the voice of the Lord strikes with flashes of lightning. The voice of the Lord shakes the desert…the voice of the Lord twists the oaks and strips the forest bare…"

And then it says this:

> "The Lord sits enthroned over the flood; the Lord is enthroned as King forever. The Lord gives strength to his people; the Lord blesses his people with peace."

What an interesting turn in Scripture. We go from the Lord's massive display of power just by his voice to bestowing strength and peace to his people. The strength and peace he offers is incomparable to anything this world can offer.

That is the God we serve.

A Friend on Your Side

What happened behind your eyes?
Where did the sparkle go?
Empty pools of sulky gray
Replace what used to be hope.

His chair, his corner of the world,
A chasm of pain stretches between
Her chair and empty word search books
What would you really search for if you
Knew you could find it?

A shoulder to lean on
An arm to shelter you
An embrace that comforts
A friend on your side.

Smother those who try to care
Look for love, look anywhere
Pop a pill and kill the pain
Wake up tomorrow, start over again.

And what would you change if you had…

A shoulder to lean on
An arm to shelter you
An embrace that comforts
A friend on your side.

I broke through barriers
Beyond all time and space.
I left the angels singing
To meet you face-to-face.

I see what's there behind your eyes
I see the sparkle is gone
Replaced with empty pools of gray
What once was trust and hope.

And I have come to be…

A shoulder to lean on
An arm to shelter you
An embrace that comforts
A friend on your side.

"I will never leave you or forsake you." Jesus

A Wee Little Man

Have you ever been in a situation where you wanted an up-close-and-personal experience with someone but you were just one person in a sea of people and couldn't get close enough? This happened to my sister and me. We had tickets to see country music artist Tim McGraw. For most of the concert, he was quite a distance from us. After one song, the stage went dark and we all waited in anticipation. All of a sudden, we could hear his voice singing but couldn't see him until a spotlight came on and illuminated him on a mini-stage right behind us! My sister was so excited she almost knocked me over! (We still laugh about that!)

What is it about our fascination with the "rich and famous"? What draws us to want to know about their lives?

There is a really interesting story in the Bible about a man doing what he needed to do to see "the star of the show."

Have you ever heard the children's song about Zacchaeus that goes like this…

"Zacchaeus was a wee little man, a wee little man was he. He climbed up in a sycamore tree for the Lord he wanted to see."

I've always thought that song was funny as a child. I'm not sure why. Maybe it was the thought of a man climbing a tree or that he was a little man. Somehow, that song directed my thoughts to *what* this man was doing instead of *why*.

As an adult, this story has so much more significance.

Two things that are important to know about Zacchaeus is that he was a chief tax collector and he was very wealthy. He would not be a man that people would respect. In fact, he would be despised. But, true to Jesus and his character, he encounters Zacchaeus on a heart level. He knows his heart before he speaks a word.

Luke 19:3 says "He (Zacchaeus) wanted to see who Jesus was…" Jesus was someone who was making a stir in his day. Not because he was rich or famous by the world's standard. Zacchaeus was on a mission to meet this man he had heard about. He became a seeker. He put himself directly in the path of Jesus, but not in a conventional way. The Bible tells us he ran ahead to get himself positioned for the passing of Jesus. Just picture that. A dignified wealthy man, picking up the skirt of his robe and running, would qualify him as "undignified." But he doesn't stop there. He finds a sycamore tree and begins to climb it.

I can just hear people in the crowd. "Was that Zacchaeus the tax collector up in that tree? Has he gone mad?"

At this point, we have Jesus mingling in with the crowd, but the moment he reaches the sycamore tree, the Bible says he looked up and saw Zacchaeus, positioned above him. And this is when Jesus brings Zacchaeus back down to his level. He tells Zacchaeus to come down out of the tree immediately.

Let's hit the pause button here. What was going through Zacchaeus' mind? Had he been heckled already by the many passing by? Had he been called names or called out because he was a tax collector? What was his preconceived notions about the "religious"? Did he wonder if Jesus was about to scold him? He must have been very surprised by the next words out of Jesus' mouth.

"I must stay at your house today."

What relief he must have felt. Look at his response. He came down at once and welcomed him (Jesus) gladly.

This simple invitation ignited Zacchaeus. This one encounter changed him. The Bible says people were grumbling because Jesus was choosing to be a guest in the house of a sinner. They judged this man by his station in life, but Jesus saw right into his heart. I wonder if that was the reason he stopped at the sycamore tree. I believe he had already seen the *heart* of Zacchaeus.

As Jesus reclined and the people whined, Zacchaeus stands up and makes a declaration.

"Look Lord! Here and now I give half of my possessions to the poor and if I have cheated anybody out of anything, I will pay back four times the amount."

Gasp! The crowd is silenced. And in that moment, Jesus takes the opportunity to reveal what they had all missed. "Today salvation has come to this house because this man, too, is a son of Abraham. For the Son of Man came to seek and to save the lost."

This story is packed full of hope!

Do you have someone in your life that you have prayed for over the years but they continue in a lifestyle that breaks your heart? *One encounter* with Jesus could change that.

Is that same person someone you have only observed by their behavior and not their heart? Jesus says, "I see their heart. I see they're lost. I see their sickness. That's exactly who I came to save…"

May I encourage you to pray for your loved ones to have that life-altering encounter with Jesus? If he can call a wealthy chief tax collector out of a tree, he can call our loved ones right where they are as well.

An Angel among Us?

In 1994, the show *Touched by an Angel* premiered and continued until 2003. This, among other media, seemed to raise the interest in angels. Do they really exist? Are they among us? New shows started popping up that told unexplainable stories where people were protected or helped by some being that they couldn't explain.

I wondered just how much angelic activity was actually going on around us. It's not new to the Christian. Angels pop up all over in the Bible in all ways, shapes, and forms. I believe in the spiritual realm. I just wasn't sure how or if it was touching the dimension and time we live in now.

One particular Sunday, I was attending church services. Our congregation had just lost one of its foundational members who helped start the church. Harold was known by all as the epitome of the godly man. He was respected and loved by all. On this particular Sunday, we were honoring his life in our service.

During one of the songs, a voice joined in with ours that was nothing short of angelic. It transported you into a place of worship. The rise and fall of this woman's voice carried all of our voices along like nothing I have ever heard before. Everything in me wanted to turn around and see where this woman was sitting.

After the service, several of us figured out who it was coming from and we approached her. She was with a man and a child and no one had ever seen them before. After they left, we all headed to the public memorial service for Harold and she was the talk of all who had heard her. We all had had the same feeling of being among something or someone "otherworldly."

No one has ever seen her again.

Was she an angel among us? Come to celebrate the life of a man who had given so much of himself for the work of the Lord? I don't know.

But I do know it was a voice of worship I will never forget. I began wondering what it will be like to be in the presence of a multitude of angels praising and singing to the King of kings.

> "Then I looked and heard the voice of many angels, numbering thousands upon thousands, and ten thousand times ten thousand. They encircled the throne…in a loud voice they were saying (singing?) 'Worthy is the Lamb who was slain, to receive power and wealth and wisdom and strength and honor and glory and praise!'" (Rev. 5:11–12).

Now, that is going to be one worship service I can't wait to hear!

Bargaining with God

Have you ever watched a movie and heard the words "God, if you save me from this, I will serve you the rest of my life! I promise!" Usually this declaration is made tongue in cheek. Life goes on and the promise disappears when the problem disappears.

The Bible tells the fascinating story of Hannah in the book of 1 Samuel. As we dig into the story, let's see if we can make sense of this woman's tenacity to be faithful.

The story begins with the introduction of Elkanah who had two wives: Hannah and Peninnah. Hannah was barren but Peninnah had children. Year after year, Peninnah would provoke Hannah to tears about her barrenness. The Bible says, "She provoked her to irritate her," and Hannah would be so upset that she couldn't even eat. So, the first thing we learn about Hannah is that she was wounded repeatedly in her most painful place, her barrenness.

The second thing we learn is that her husband did not understand her pain. He asks, "Why are you downhearted? Don't I mean more to you than ten sons?" Oops, missed her heart big time on that one. But what does Hannah do with her bitter disappointment? Often we as wives put a demand on our husbands to "get us," don't we? Not Hannah. We are told that, in her deep anguish, she prayed to the Lord, weeping bitterly. Hannah knew that God was the *only* person capable of hearing her deepest desire, which was to remove her shame. She knew if he opened her womb to conceive a child, her status would change in the community.

It was in this state of mind that she bargains with God. First Samuel 1:11 says, And she made a vow, saying, "Lord Almighty, if you will only look on your servant's misery and remember me, and not forget your servant but give her a son, then I will give him to the Lord for all the days of his life…"

But Hannah was misunderstood again. Eli the priest saw her mouth moving as she prayed and thought she was drunk!

Have you ever been misunderstood in your own pain/shame? Or, have you ever misunderstood someone in their pain/shame? We are told that Hannah was "praying in her heart." Who can possibly know our heart that intimately but God alone? Who is capable of tenderly caring for our wounded hearts like God? Hannah knew this. She told Eli, "I was pouring out my soul to the Lord."

And something happened when she did this. Her belief in God's loving care motivated her out of her grief! How?

1. She took her grief to the One who deeply understood her pain.
2. She prayed in her rawness. She was real before God.
3. She received encouragement from Eli the priest.
4. She gave over *all* to God, trusting him alone.
5. She didn't wait until he answered her prayer. She did this while she was still barren *and* still being taunted by Peninnah.

Verse 19 tells us "the Lord remembered her." Not only did the Lord bless her, he gave her the greater blessing—a son! That is so like God. We ask for good things and he delivers great things!

Now this is where the story gets really interesting. Hannah, we are told, bonded with her son Samuel before keeping her promise to give him up. The average age of a child being weaned from his nursing mother was three years old.

Just think about that. If you have children, think about all that would transpire between you in those first three years. Samuel would just be on the threshold of a full life, and a promise by his mother was going to sweep her out of his life. As we read further, we have every reason to become pro-Hannah and support her going back on her word. If I were Hannah, I would have certainly gone back to the bargaining table.

These three reasons would be good enough for me.

- We learn that Eli's sons were "scoundrels" and they had no regard for the Lord. I don't know about you, but Eli's parenting resume would not sit well with me.
- Surely God would be okay with her changing her mind, right? After all, she *is* the mother of Samuel. What child wouldn't benefit from being raised by his own loving mother?
- Hannah is a woman. Women/mothers are natural nurturers. Wouldn't that be best for Samuel?

From our perspective, God's plan seems backward. But from God's perspective, he knew the future of Samuel's life. We read that "the boy Samuel continued to grow in stature and in favor with the Lord and with people."

So, this story begs to ask this question: When we enter into a relationship with God and he tells us to trust him even when it makes no sense, do we bargain or do we bow?

"Come let us bow down and kneel before the Lord our God, our Maker."

Bring It in Close

I am not a very sporty person. I will watch sports, but I've never had much interest in playing them. That is, until I had a grandson. He loves anything to do with a ball. Kicking it, running with it, throwing it. So, when he says, "Gramma, will you play football with me and Papa?" how do I say no?

We were out in the yard getting ready for our big two-on-one game and I was teamed up with Cole. He was huddled with me, telling me what I needed to do for the play to be successful, but he was using "football" terms. I just thought the only thing I needed to know was start running, try to catch the ball, and keep it tucked in close to me. After several blotched attempts, Cole realized I was the rookie on the team.

The next time he came over, he brought a new football. As we were sitting at the kitchen table, he said, "Gramma, I bought this football for you. See, it has all the plays on it so you will know what to do." I was so touched by his deep longing to have me be a part of his world. He was trying to make it easier for me to fit into it.

So out we went again. And, even with all the plays written on the ball, I still narrowed down my job to three things: run, catch, and bring the ball in close.

There is something about carrying something in a protective closeness that feels…right.

I think about the different ways I can carry something. I can carry a handbag from my hand or on my shoulder. I can tuck mail up under my armpit. I can sling a backpack on my back. But when it comes to something very, very precious to me, I pull it in close to me, nestled against my heart. Think about a card or letter you receive that speaks volumes to you. It evokes a tender emotion and you hold it close to your heart as the tears fall. Or think about a little child who just wants to be close to you for a snuggle or a hug. You bend your body all the way around them and don't want to let go.

Maybe that's why I find joy in this verse from Isaiah 40:11: "He tends His flock like a shepherd. He gathers the lambs in His arms and carries them close to His heart."

What a lovely picture. Can you find comfort in knowing that the Lord delights in holding you close this way? Close to his very heart? I can't think of a safer place to be. It's where we belong.

Broken Branches

Sometimes you just have to take a walk and get alone with God. I was walking around a ski resort because that's what people do when they don't ski and everyone else in the family does! I was wandering aimlessly on a path in the woods, looking for God in the simple things. Since it was winter and everything around me was either dead or without color, there wasn't much to look at.

But God uses even the ugly and withered things of the wintry season. I looked over and saw a cracked tree branch, broken but fallen into the embrace of another tree. It seems that God uses wood quite often to speak to us.

I was reminded that, even though I am broken, when I fall, he is there to catch me.

And it also reminded me that, 2,000 years ago, Jesus saved me from another fall. Adam and Eve took a disastrous step out of God's provision of the Garden of Eden, and it broke the rest of history. That is, until Jesus said, "I am willing to break my body against a wooden cross as a sacrifice for all."

Plain, rough, and splintered wood seems to be the Carpenter's choice to speak to us, then and now.

Be Still… No, Really, Be Still

(A Conversation between God and Me)

Me: My mind is in motion.
God: Then you're not being still.

Me: My heart is churning.
God: Then you're not being still.

Me: I want to know.
God: Know what? That I am God?

Me: Well, that too.
God: What else is there you need to know?

Me: Well, there must be more than just knowing You are God.
God: Like?

Me: Like, why You seem to keep some of Your promises but not all of them?
God: Are you sure about that?

Me: Well, it seems that way. Five years seems like an awful long time for my sister to battle depression without any answers.
God: How do you know I'm not answering?

Me: She's not back to the sister I once knew.
God: And how do you know I'm not refining a new Joan?

Me: I guess I don't, but it sure looks a lot more like a hopeless situation than a refining one.
God: That's because you can only see the broken pot of clay and not the Master Potter mending behind the scenes.

Me: Well, I want to see what You see.
God: No, you don't.

Me: Why not?
God: Because then you couldn't do what you are supposed to do and let me do what I alone am capable of doing.

Me: What's that supposed to be?
God: (smiling). Be still.

Me: Oh, that.
God: Yes, that. I *alone* am God.

Beyond a Look-See

All of us have undoubtedly seen a man or woman sitting by the side of the road holding a sign asking for help because they are homeless and in great need of something. And, undoubtedly, most of us see this person and we look the other way. For whatever reason, it's too uncomfortable; we don't trust the situation or we don't have time for another's unfortunate circumstances.

Not my friend Tammy. She was out and about shopping to provide for her family. As she left the parking lot of a store, she spotted a man sitting at a light with a sign begging for help. She felt a jolt of compassion in her heart for him. I suppose many of us get to this point and then we move on with our day. Here's where the story gets really good.

Tammy's compassion for this man went beyond her own. She felt the compassion of her loving Father for this man so she went and bought him a meal, got out of her car, approached him, and then *sat down* next to him and asked him one simple question, "Tell me your story."

This opened the floodgates for this man to share his journey. I'm certain that he saw something in my friend's eyes that were beyond her. I am certain he was experiencing a loving touch from a loving God, whether he knew it or not.

Jesus often did the same thing in his word. In Matthew 9, we read the story of a woman who had been bleeding for twelve years, most likely marginalized from her community and needing a loving touch. She was so embarrassed by her condition that, when she saw Jesus, she knew enough about him that she was certain if she snuck up behind him and just touched his cloak, she would be healed. She would also be aware that she would defile Jesus if she touched him because of her condition and what the Law said.

Here's where *this* story gets good. The Bible records these five words of hope for us.

"Jesus turned and saw her" (Matt. 9:22).

Jesus acknowledged this woman who had tried to live in the shadows, unable to rise above her need because of shame. The Bible says she sought medical help, exhausting all her financial resources, but just got worse. In her hopelessness, she went into hiding.

Until she was completely exposed and face-to-face with the only cure. Jesus saw her. He saw more than just her face. He saw her fatigue. He saw more than just her ailment. He saw her agony. He saw more than just her shunning. He saw her shame.

He turned and *saw* her.

And he had compassion on her.

> "Daughter, your faith has healed you. Go in peace and be freed from your suffering" (Mark 5:34).

This is such a beautiful picture of Jesus offering more than just a look-see.

First, he calls her daughter. He acknowledges an intimate relationship with her.

Secondly, he heals her because of her faith. But he doesn't just offer a quick "meal for the moment." He invites her to tell her story. And she does.

Mark 5:33 says, "The woman, knowing what had happened to her, came and fell at his feet and, trembling with fear, told him the *whole truth*."

Then he sends her back to her life with a new offer of peace and freedom, two things that were eluding her because of her physical condition.

What is that one thing that is causing you such grief right now that you need just a touch from the Master's hand? Do you believe that he wants to come and "sit down" with you and ask you, "What's your story?" He does. He cares that intimately about you.

Let him have a look-see. A really long, lifetime look-see.

Can Sin Ever Be Cute?

We have all heard how ugly sin can be. It can destroy and rob and debilitate the strongest of God's creation. But I wonder, can sin ever be "cute"? Most would say those two words just can't be in the same sentence. Then this happened…

My husband was taking some time with our sons to do a bedtime devotional when they were young. He was talking to them about what sin is. To engage them, he asked *them* to give examples of what *they* thought sin is. As they each gave their child's version of what sin meant to them, our youngest decided to *show* what sin looks like. He took off his slipper and said, "I know this is a sin," and whipped the slipper at my husband, connecting smack dab in the face!

My husband lost it and broke out in laughter.

I suppose that sinful behavior from a child can be cute, but they don't stay children. Those little rebellious beings become big rebellious beings. And those big rebellious beings learn to throw more than slippers in our face. They learn to throw words in our face that sting, or even greater, they expose *our* sin and can throw that in our faces. That hurts. Truth often does.

So the next time you are face-to-face (literally) with a child's rebellious behavior, see it for what it really is. A great teaching moment.

> "Train up a child in the way he should go
> and when he is old he will not depart from it"
> (Prov. 22:6).

God calls us to "train up" our children. And yet, many parents, including myself, have done this and watched their child depart from their teaching. I find it interesting that the verse just prior to this one says, "In the paths of the wicked are snares and pitfalls, but those who would preserve their life stay far from them."

Our children can be molded, but they cannot be controlled by us. We can lead. We can instruct. As one speaker shared at a seminar on parenting, "God calls us to be godly parents. This does not guarantee godly children."

If we question that thought, we only need to look at our own bent toward sin. How many times have you or I chosen something, *anything*, over God's parental leading? If we are honest, it would be a daily thing. Sometimes throwing a slipper, or a tantrum, just plain feels good.

I just hope that we can be grace extenders like our Heavenly Father when we face the rebellion of our children. That, and learn how to duck quicker!

Dogged by a Movie

I am not a dog lover. I'm just not. Maybe getting bit in the face when I was a toddler gave me a mistrust of them. Or maybe growing up with dogs and discovering later that I have an allergy to some took away any enthusiasm for these four-legged creatures.

Either way, I was completely surprised when I fell in love with a movie about dogs. In the movie, called *Eight Below*, a man and team set out for the frozen wasteland of Antarctica with a team of sled dogs. Due to horrific weather conditions and an accident, the team is forced to leave the area, leaving the dogs behind, with the intention of coming back for them right away. To make sure the dogs can't get loose and run away, Jerry, their owner, tightens their collars that are attached to a chain line. The harsh winter lingers on and they are not able to return as planned, and the dogs' owner is grieved over leaving them behind, facing their certain death.

It isn't until the following spring that he is able to return to the base where the dogs were tied up. The line they were secured to is buried in the snow and when Jerry pulls on it, thinking they are all still attached and dead, he realizes they have freed themselves except for the oldest dog. He looks out over the vast wintry expanse and, in that moment, he hears the faint sound of barking. Could it be true? Has one of the dogs survived?

As he heads to the horizon, not only does he see one, but five of his dogs running toward him. He scoops them up in his arms, full of joy that they survived. As they pack up the dogs to return home, he glances back at the horizon, sad for the loss of the three remaining dogs.

Max, one of the dogs, will not get into the vehicle and runs off. Jerry takes off after him. Max leads him to Maya, another one of the dogs, lying in the snow, weak but alive. Jerry scoops her up in his arms and then we see the rest of the team locked on the horizon, wondering what they will see, when Jerry comes over the hill, carrying his beloved dog.

This scene gets me every time. Why? Why am I so moved?

It reminds me that I also have been in shackles, left on my own to die, but there was *someone* who loved me too much to leave me here on my own. Jesus decided to do whatever it took, including a vicious death, to get to me because he longs that *none* should perish.

It reminds me that he came seeking what is his, little ol' me, who was lost and carries me in his arms back to safety again.

> "The Lord himself goes before you and will be with you; he will never leave you nor forsake you. Do not be afraid; do not be discouraged" (Deut. 31:8).

Can We Ever Be Satisfied?

As I think about the word "satisfied," I wonder, "What truly brings satisfaction?" Is there something outside myself, my circumstances, my desires, the things that I possess, that bring satisfaction to my core? I can honestly say I have felt deep satisfaction in many things of this world. And yet, as quickly as I can admit that, I also have to admit that most, if not all of the things that came to mind, did not have the power to *keep* me satisfied. The shine would wear off, the desire would fade for a new desire, and the search would start all over again.

That's why I love this verse from Psalm 90:14. "Satisfy us in the morning with your unfailing love, that we may sing for joy and be glad *all* our days."

Starting off my day with a deep, eternal satisfaction in a love that blows all other desires out of the water, I find my feet get set right for the day. I looked up the definition of the word "satisfaction" and some of the synonyms are contentment, fulfillment, enjoyment. Every single one of these words accurately describe the love of the Savior. I feel more content when I am enjoying the fulfillment of his love.

> Lord of Heaven,
>
> Each day I wake I am more and more aware of the necessity to fall into your vision of what it means to live life to the fullest. Each day I must trust you have given me a purpose to bring glory to your name. There are some days when I struggle to see what that purpose is. When this is my waking thought, redirect my steps. I give you each day, Lord, from the moment I open my

eyes. Do not let me take one step that doesn't have me walking in step with you. Do with each day you give me what you will. I pray that my eyes would be keenly aware and watching for whatever it might be that you have planned for my day.

I pray I would be content in whatever you give me each day. I pray that my actions would match my heart and that you would strip me of a calloused or cynical heart. Fill my heart with your joy so that I might sing of your praise from morning 'til night.

Change my heart, God. I will be satisfied in you, and you alone.

Dreaming Out Loud

Like most men, my husband is not a shopper. He would be completely satisfied if I put a list in his hand at Christmas so he could dash in and out of a store. But there have been times when he wanted to surprise me, so he became what I would call a "sneaky shopper." He begins to listen for hints of things I would like to have when I am unaware that he is listening. This can mostly work to his advantage, but there have been a few times when it backfired. I often see and express beauty in things, but it doesn't necessarily mean I want to own them. I am also a frugal shopper so I will often pass on something that I would never pay the asking price. Sometimes I am just "dreaming out loud." I learned real fast not to do that around my husband at Christmastime.

This played out in an interesting way with David and his men when they were at battle against the Philistines. David did his own "dreaming out loud." He remembered calmer days and fond memories of his time while in Bethlehem. And in that moment of remembering, he said, "Oh that someone would get me a drink of water from the well near the gate of Bethlehem!"

Three of David's warriors were listening. And like my husband wanting to please me, they wanted to please their king. So much so, they risked their lives to break through the Philistine lines, retrieve water, and bring it back to King David.

Okay, let's just pretend we are walking along with these valiant men, who have sworn to give their lives to protect their king, and who have just risked their lives to bring him a cool drink of water. I imagine they were pretty pumped with adrenaline and couldn't wait to be honored with words or action when they bowed down before David and presented him with the water he so desired.

What happens next leaves us scratching our heads.

"But he (David) refused to drink it; instead, he poured it out before the Lord. 'Far be it from me, Lord, to do this!' he said. 'Is this not the blood of men who went at the risk of their lives?' And David would not drink it."

What was *that* all about?

I'm pretty certain that David loved and respected his men. I don't think he was intentionally asking them to go into battle, risking their lives, for a simple drink of water. I believe he was speaking more rhetorically, conveying his desire for *all* of Bethlehem to once again be free from the rule of the Philistines, including the freedom to drink from the well at the gate.

So, we read, that he "poured it out before the Lord." He knew that the Lord had been involved in protecting these three men when they went behind enemy lines. It became a drink offering.

Have you ever been that desperate to please Jesus? Has there ever been a request made by him that you wanted to honor so badly that you were willing to risk everything to please him? Has he asked you to rush into any battle of life with no thought of yourself other than securing his living water for your life? Whether he has spoken subtly or directly to you, what would keep you from honoring his request?

Jesus found each of us worthy of sacrifice. What would our lives look like if we did the same for him?

Dream Big

I have been thinking how I've had you in a box
And in my mind I've limited you
I need to set you free
Allowing you to be
The God who cannot be contained.

Dream big, your dreams won't disappear
Hope big, in him our hope is clear
He's promised us more than we
Could imagine or ask,
Our God, he is able to rise to the task.
Dream big.

Sometimes my eyes see the world full of pain
And it troubles my weary heart
But my eyes need to be
Fixed only on thee
The God who will not be restrained.

Pray big, he hears each spoken prayer
Love big, for the world needs love that's rare.
He's promised us more than we could imagine or ask
Our God, he is able to rise to the task.
Pray big.

Sometimes I wonder if I'm really heard
Or is it you I hear when reading your Word?
Then you burst forth from pages

As *thee* Rock of ages
The God who says, "I will remain."

Ask big, he offers his kingdom to you
Share big, the Christ who can make all things new
He promised us more than we could imagine or ask
Our God, he is able to rise to the task.
Ask big.

Dream big
Hope big
Pray big
Love big
Ask big
Share big
Our God, he cannot be contained,
Our God who will not be restrained,
Our God who says "I will remain."

Everlasting Gobstoppers

Mix together imagination, children, and sweets and what do you get? Willy Wonka and the Chocolate Factory. It's one of those classics that speaks into the hearts of children of all ages. I remember the first time I really thought about Willy Wonka's creation, the Everlasting Gobstopper. He claimed that no amount of sucking on this piece of candy would diminish it. It would last forever and ever. Each child eagerly put out their hand to receive such an amazing sweet. They had eternal taste-bud satisfaction being offered before their very eyes.

I think of all the things I just had to have, only to find it stuffed in a corner of my basement or bagged up for a Salvation Army run. I think of all the activities, relationships, promises that have come and gone. And it stirs the deep longing of my heart that secretly cries out, "Does *anything* ever last?" Is there anything eternal that, once tasted, would bring that much satisfaction?

Then I read the words from Jeremiah 31:3. God says, "I have loved you with an *everlasting* love."

That's pretty incredible when you think about who is saying those words. This is God, who knows every intimate detail of our hearts, every dusty corner and deceitful motive. This is God, who created us to be in his image and watched as we walked away from his perfect plan into sin. This is God, who sees what we were created for and capable of. He sees it all and still he says, "I love you with an everlasting, *eternal* love."

What could be more satisfying than that? Jesus died to give me everlasting life, and it is always, always entwined with everlasting love.

One taste of God's love. It's amazingly sweet. And it never, ever runs out.

Flying Fudge

The Grand Hotel on Mackinac Island in Michigan is quite frankly…grand! It's one of my favorite places to go if I want to experience the royal treatment. You just get caught up in being transferred back to a time when you arrived by carriage in all your fineries and were recognized as someone worthy of rolling out the red carpet. Even to this day, if you are a guest at the Grand Hotel, you are treated like a dignitary. They even have a formal dress code around the dinner hour. However, prior to that, you can be on the grounds in your everyday clothes.

On one such visit with my sister, we had gone downtown to do a little shopping. Mackinac Island is known for their fudge. My sister had purchased some and we headed back to the Grand to get ready for our evening. We took a shortcut through the gardens on the lower level of the grounds, which put us at the stairs right across from the massive entrance, still donned with red carpet.

Now, this area is also the staging area for the fancy carriage of the Grand Hotel. There sat the coachman atop of the carriage, waiting for his next passengers. Because the carriage is up higher, he can pull up to the end of the step, which is also higher, to collect his guests.

I don't know if it was being so enamored by the "grand-ness" of the Grand Hotel, or just a misjudgment, but as my sister approached the "red carpet," her foot caught the high step and she went flying face down on the red carpet, hanging on as best she could to her fudge. I looked over at the coachman and he was just shaking his head. I guess he's seen this before!

Of course I was the sympathetic sister who couldn't contain her laughter and was secretly thanking God that it was her and not me splayed out for all to see.

But, oh, the many times I have approached God just like this. I come to his throne with my grip on things I just have to hang on to, like that fudge, and he's saying, "Watch your step if you are going to make that worry/fear/shame more important than my invitation up the red carpet into My Presence. It's going to be your downfall."

What's that one thing you are hanging on to that causes you to stumble when you come into the presence of God? What is keeping you from staying upright and trusting him to guide your steps? What keeps you from coming to him in confidence?

Hebrews 4:16 says, "Let us then approach God's throne of grace with confidence, so that we may receive mercy and find grace to help us in our time of need."

He's not like that coachman who just shakes his head when we have stumbled. He's the Master of Ceremonies waiting to seat you at the big banquet feast going on. *You* are his dignitary because of the finished work of his son, Jesus. Go! Enjoy him! And guess what? You don't have to get fancied up like you do at the Grand. You can come just as you are!

Face Planted in the Father's Hand

My husband and I were on vacation and some locals told us to check out a restaurant that was known for its homemade Polish food. After traveling through the infamous Tunnel of Trees in Michigan, we came upon the Legs Inn. After we were seated, I noticed a young family of five at a table near us. I noted how well behaved all the children were, how attentive the parents were to each of them. The father was holding his youngest child, who was obviously ready for naptime. He could barely keep his eyes open.

As we waited to be served, I couldn't stop watching this child and his father. He would take his face and plant it in his father's hand, then wrap his other arm around his daddy. What was interesting was every time the father would remove his hand, the child would stir and seek it out again and bring it back to his face, resting his head in his father's hand. There was a sweet security this child found in the embrace and support of his father.

It was such a beautiful picture of how we should position ourselves with our Heavenly Father.

When we are tired and weary, rest in his hands for support.

When we are afraid or lonely, rest in his hands for comfort.

When we are uncertain about the future, rest in his hands for security.

I love how God speaks into this in Isaiah 41:10. "So do not fear, for I am with you; do not be dismayed, for I am your God. I will strengthen you and help you; I will uphold you with my righteous right hand."

Lord Jesus, cover us with your loving and strong hands. Teach us to seek you for care and comfort. Help us position ourselves in your security and find sweet moments knowing you've got us. Thank you for being such an involved Father. Amen.

God Is Not Finished... Even When He Says He Is

Jesus said, "It is finished." John 19:30

I have heard these three words for most of my life. And I know at the very moment they were spoken, the greatest sacrifice ever made was complete. Jesus took every sin, *every single sin all at the same time*, and *crushed* them... He got face-to-face and nose-to-nose with the enemy and with burning passion in his eyes, and us on his mind, he said, "You have *no power* here." He won the battle. His death on the cross and resurrection from the grave was the finishing blow.

So we might step into life thinking we have a cake walk before us. We can have what we want, do what we want, crave and collect, and in doing so, we miss *life*. We miss what Jesus began and what he ended. We miss that his sacrifice ended the *power* of sin, but we also miss that it began the *presence* of his power.

"It is finished." Such a tiny word. *It*. What does *it* encompass? More than we will ever know or understand because only an Almighty God and Savior could ever endure the entire weight of the sin of the world and come out the other end standing.

And not just standing but seated at the right hand of the Father, ready to watch his second greatest gift continue the work of what he finished.

> "And with that he breathed on them and
> said, 'Receive the Holy Spirit.'" John 20:22

If all was finished, then why did he have to send the Holy Spirit? His great work *was* finished, but he is not finished with *us*...yet. He didn't just return to heaven and leave us to figure this all out. He lovingly left his Spirit. It begins as a tiny spark in the very heart of us and it bursts forth when *we* say, "God, I'm finished fighting these battles on my own. I can't do this anymore. I need you."

Boom! He sets his Spirit deep within our heart as an everlasting light that cannot be extinguished. He took every thought, every fear, every doubt, every single enemy of the Cross and *crushed* them! And those spirits of darkness are angry. Oh they are not giving us up that easily.

Swords are coming out. Bloody battles have begun.

> "What then shall we say in response to these things? If God is for us, who can be against us? He who did not spare his own Son, but gave him up for us all—how will he not also, *along with him*, graciously give us all things? Who will bring any charge against those whom God has chosen? It is God who justifies. Who then is the one who condemns? *No one*!" (Rom. 8:31–34).

Did you catch that? *No one*! Not even ourselves! Keep reading!

> "Christ Jesus who died—more than that" (um, pause, how could there possibly be more than that?) "who was raised to life—is at the right hand of God and is *also* interceding for us. Who shall separate us from the love of Christ? Shall trouble or hardship or persecution or famine or nakedness or danger or sword? ...*No*! In all these things we are more than conquerors through him who loved us" (Rom. 8:34–35, 37)

He is *not* finished.

Following the Light in Droves

On August 21, 2017, you could not pick up a newspaper or turn on a news broadcast without hearing about a mass exodus of people across the US. Some people traveled hundreds of miles to get in the pathway of a phenomenon. They packed up their cars and campers and turned their eyes to the skies. For a *two-minute* event!

What was going on?

A rare solar eclipse.

Reports said it was the most viewed solar eclipse in history! Hotels and motels in the path of the eclipse were booked solid.

Could you imagine if the headlines read, "A rare viewing will happen this very day. Come and see! I am the Light; in me there is no darkness at all. Come, see the Light of life! Come see your God!"

Jesus Christ *is* eternal radiance! Nothing can extinguish the Glory of the Lord!

Like many of us who only experienced a partial solar eclipse, for now, we only see partially what will be revealed in full when the Lord returns. His Glory is rare. It shone at the Cross and it will shine again fully when we see him face-to-face. Ready for a road trip?

He's Not Here

For a short period of my life, I became a part of a growing group of mothers...the working mother. I have nothing against mothers who work outside of the home. It just wasn't what I would choose. All my life I wanted to be a stay-at-home mom. But then a divorce put me in a situation that required me to go back to work.

I began the search for a daycare for my two-year-old son. There wasn't a day that I dropped him off that I didn't feel the agony of leaving him with someone else to care for him. I was missing out on what I *wanted* to be my job and calling. I wanted to be the one to shape his formative years. He was my heart.

I developed a friendship with Cheryl, one of the caretakers at the daycare. It eased some of my worry and concerns for my son. I knew he was in good hands with this young woman.

On one particular day, I was at work and I received a phone call from the daycare. They told me that two men had come and asked for my son by name (but they pronounced it wrong), saying that they were there to pick him up. Thinking quickly, Cheryl said there was another daycare in the area and maybe that is where they needed to go. They left and she immediately called me. I panicked! I told her I was leaving work immediately to head her way. That half-hour drive was one of the longest drives I've ever experienced. I couldn't get there fast enough to see my son and be his protection from these men. I had no idea who they were, but I had a pretty good idea who was behind this. After all, I was in the middle of a custody battle.

When I got to the daycare, I flew out of my car and ran to the door. Cheryl greeted me immediately and then she said these three words. "He's not here."

These three simple words rocked my world.

Push a pause button for a minute.

I want to share with you another story that rocked the *whole* world. Same three words.

> "On the first day of the week, very early in the morning, the women took the spices they had prepared and went to the tomb. They found the stone rolled away from the tomb but when they entered, they did not find the body of the Lord Jesus. While they were wondering about this, suddenly two men in clothes that gleamed like lightning stood beside them. In their fright the women bowed down with their faces to the ground, but the men said to them, 'Why do you look for the living among the dead? *He's not here!*'" (Luke 24:1–6).

How tragic if my story or this story in Luke, stopped with these words. But, both stories continue.

> "He has risen, just as he said!" (Luke 24:6).

It's why we can celebrate Easter like no one else.
Our God is *raised*.

> "Christ died for our sins…was buried, then raised on the third day according to the Scriptures and then appeared to Peter, then to the twelve and after that, he appeared to more than five hundred of the brothers at the same time" (1 Cor. 15:3–6).

Our God is *real*.

> "There is *one* God and *one* mediator between God and men, the man Christ Jesus, who gave himself as a ransom for all men." (1 Tim. 2:5–6).

Our God is *relational*.

> "My Father's house has many rooms... I am going there to prepare a place for you. And if I go and prepare a place for you, I will come back and take you to be with me that you also may be where I am" (John 14:2–3).

The death and resurrection of Jesus Christ *rocked* the world and changed it forever.

And, as Paul Harvey used to say, "Now, for the rest of the story."

After I heard "He's not here," I was told that my fiancé had picked up my son from school. My son was safe. He was alive! As for those two men who came looking for him, well, that's another story.

Hanging with the What Ifs and If Onlys

I love one-on-one time with a friend. It's so intimate and focused. There is no concern wondering if another person is feeling left out. It's just the two of us bantering back and forth. At least, I have thought it was just the two of us.

Have you ever thought about the "unseen" guests that sneak through your door when you have someone over? They might not have been invited by you or your guest, but they slip in unnoticed.

And they are not our friends. They are as noisy and distractive as if we had invited a whole houseful of people. We know them by name. And they show up more often than we are aware. Just listen to this conversation.

You: It's so good to finally sit down with you and be able to catch up!
Friend: I know! It's been way too long. Life has been so busy. How
    does that happen that so much time slips away between visits.
You: So tell me what's been going on with your family.

Your friend begins to share about their children, husband, work or the situation that is consuming them.

And that's when those unseen guests enter the conversation.

Friend: And then my husband told me that he was going to lose his
    bonus this year.
If Only: If only he would've planned for our retirement better. We
    wouldn't have to worry so much about our finances.
What If: What if we lose our house or don't have the resources to take
    care of our medical needs?

You: Oh you are not alone in worrying about your future. It's tough today to have financial security.

Friend: Oh, and did I tell you about Sally? She's moving in with her boyfriend.

If Only: If only I could convince her that's a really bad decision. I wish she would realize how damaging that can be to her heart. It just makes me worry about her.

What If: What if he breaks her heart? I know what that feels like. What if she gets pregnant? What if…? What if…? What if…?

You: These kids these days. No one ever tells us how to relate to adult children. They think we don't know what we are talking about. As if we haven't lived through our own mistakes.

If Only: If only I could go back and correct the mistakes I made. I just want to protect her from making some of the same mistakes.

What If: I want to tell her about how Jesus has changed my life, but what if she rejects me and even worse, rejects Jesus? I just don't know if I could live with that!

You: We sure live with a lot of regret and worry. Maybe we need to let go of those and pray about these things.

Friend: You're right. Why is that always the last thing I think about doing?

> "Don't *worry* about anything; instead, pray about everything. Tell God what you need, and thank him for all he has done. *Then* you will experience God's peace, which exceeds anything we can understand. His peace will guard your hearts and minds as you live in Christ Jesus" (Phil. 4:6–7).

I don't know about you, but I think I need to change up my guest list a bit. I'm kicking out Ms. What If and Ms. If Only, and I'm going to invite the new neighbors, Ms. Trust and Ms. Peace. They always bring something every visit that makes the day a whole lot richer and rewarding!

I See Your True Colors

I live in a four-season state. Each season has its own unique beauty. I am particularly fond of autumn. The visual display of colors, the smells and sounds of leaves crackling, the cool nights as we say goodbye for now to summer. The funny thing is, everything I just described is a description of death.

Every time I ooh and aah over the brilliance of bright orange, red, and crimson leaves, I am soaking in death. It is the natural cycle of life going to seed so that another season, spring, will produce new life.

Jesus talks about this just before he is arrested and sent to his death. In John 12:24, he said, "Very truly I tell you, unless a kernel of wheat falls to the ground and dies, it remains only a single seed. But if it dies, it produces many seeds."

God does the same thing with us. You've heard the saying, "We go through seasons of life"? It's so true! There are times when God refines our character but never before he calls us to die to self. We need our "winters," those times of being in the season of waiting, for something new to be produced in us. And before we know it, new "buds" are springing forth in our character.

There is beauty in death. I think that's why Jesus made such a big deal about it.

> "See, I am making all things new!" (Rev. 21:5).

Heart Burn

Cool autumn days and hot soup just go together. I was out shopping at the mall and decided to pop into a restaurant for a bowl of soup. I dipped into the thick, creamy delight before me and took my first bite. That's when it hit me. The soup was extremely hot and I had already done the damage. I burned the roof of my mouth. I'm not talking about a stinging temporary burn from neglecting to blow on the soup to cool it down. I'm talking about scalding hot soup that left a pea-size hole burned in my mouth! I couldn't comfortably eat anything for over a month! Every bite of food brought me back to that intense moment.

Luke tells us his own story about a burn. Cleopas and another disciple are taking a walk to the town Emmaus. As they chatted, they were joined by Jesus, but they didn't immediately recognize him. The Bible says it was a seven-mile walk from Jerusalem. It doesn't specifically say that Jesus was walking with them the whole seven miles, but even one mile would have added some interesting conversation with a resurrected Savior! Apparently it *was* interesting because they asked Jesus to stay with them. It was during this late evening time that they recognized Jesus as he broke bread with them. Aha! His trademark!

And then he disappeared!

Such an interesting twist! Why would he finally reveal himself and then just vanish into thin air?

I think the answer is in Luke 24:32, "Were not our hearts burning within us while he talked with us on the road and opened the Scriptures to us?"

I think Jesus physically disappeared, but he left a heart burn in each of these men. He stirred them up beyond the stirrings of their emotions to the stirrings in their souls. He saw they had no peace. So what does he do? He shows up a second time, as they are sharing their experience with the other disciples. And he offers them the words they really need to hear. "Peace be with you."

And once again, they didn't realize it was Jesus in the flesh. They thought he was a ghost.

And Jesus goes back and illuminates their minds again with Scripture. And then he seals the deal with a promise that rings true for each of us this day. He reminds them that he is not leaving them empty-handed.

"I am going to send you what my Father has promised; but stay in the city until you have been clothed with power from on high" (the coming of the Holy Spirit).

No matter what road we are journeying on, who we are walking alongside, no matter what has happened in our past that is still confusing in our present, Jesus has left each of us a gift. His Spirit is here, now.

Is not our hearts burning within us when he talks to us…and opens the Scripture to us?

How is your heart burn? Really, really intense, I hope.

I Chose You

Roller-skating parties were a big deal when I was in junior high. Our whole class would go together. We would have open skate, but the whole time, my heart would be pounding because I knew "couples skate" was coming. It was one of my most exhilarating and excruciating memories as a young tween.

The rink announcer would tell all the boys to line up on one side of the rink and all the girls would line up on the opposite side. Then, one by one, a boy would come over and choose a skate partner. Each of us knew who would get chosen first, but what consumed our minds was this thought: "Will I be chosen last?" No one wanted to be the last girl waiting to be chosen.

In seventh grade, I had a huge crush on a boy named Scott. I would have done anything to be able to wrap my hand in his and do a few laps around the rink for all to see. It would have filled my love bank for a month! As the couples skate began, my eyes took quick peeks across the vast rink to see where he was waiting for his turn. Everything inside of me was screaming, "Pick me! Pick me!" And every time he would make his way to our side and couple up with another girl, my heart would sink and be destroyed.

Until midway through seventh grade.

I waited in anticipation as I always did, believing that my silent cry to be chosen would go unnoticed once again. And then, there he was. Standing in front of me, holding out his hand to me. My heart was beating so fast I almost missed the message that was in his extended hand. "I choose you."

My world was never the same after that.

This memory came flooding back to me as I read John 15:16. Jesus was speaking to his disciples and he said these words, "You did not choose me, but *I chose you...*"

Just think about that. Not only are those amazing, life-giving words for anyone to hear, but they aren't spoken by just anyone. They were spoken by Jesus.

Let that sink in. Jesus, face-to-face with you, demanding your attention so you don't miss it.

I. Chose. You

We are chosen out of love.
We are chosen out of passion for his created.
We are chosen for a purpose.

When you are standing frozen, begging the world to choose you, look up. A hand is being extended to you. He skated across time, zeroed in on *you* and says with great delight, *I choose you*!

Hull-Less

I love popcorn. I really love popcorn, but it hasn't always loved me since I have diverticulosis. Doctors told me to stay away from it. That was like death for me!

Then I took a trip to Amish country and I discovered hull-less popcorn. I was so ecstatic! Popcorn without the menacing hull that can flare up my condition. However, as I read the disclaimer on the bag, it said, "There is really no such thing as hull-less popcorn as the hull is what needs to burst open to produce the popped corn. But this particular hull is the tiniest one there is so the hull is almost nonexistent."

Almost nonexistent, but it still exists.

I liken this to the very seed of God, placed within us when we were created in his image. We don't always see that seed because we all have a condition—sin. His seed is often masked by our current sin nature.

Like popcorn, this seed needs warmth to "explode." We need the love of Jesus Christ.

Often, like popcorn, the seed within us needs to be shaken up a bit. Trials we experience often bring the "heat" necessary to produce the finished work in us. The seed within us, Jesus, *is* the finished product. Without the seed of Jesus Christ, there is no me! There cannot be a complete person if his glory doesn't burst forth from his seed.

So what is the moral of the story? Without the seed of Christ living in me, reigning in me, being the very center of my being, I am just a hull-less shell of a person.

No hull=no popcorn.
No Jesus=no bride of Christ.

Oh and by the way, when I get to the Great Banquet Feast for the Bride of Christ, if you can't find me, just look for the biggest bowl of popcorn. I'll be the one with my face planted in it!

I Wanna Be Caught

I've been drifting through life
Mostly doing as I was told
Finding ways to make life work
Then came a fork in the road.

Do I settle for what's left?
Or do I choose to live right?
I have heard I need to walk
By faith and not by sight.

Oh God, have you been chasing me?
Is it you my heart has fought?
I'm choosing not to run away
I just wanna be caught.

I sat listening to their words
Forgiveness could be mine.
They said, "Your love, it is a gift,
Today, and for all time."

The choice was mine to make, they said
It's yours and yours alone.
That's when I felt you drawing me
You said, "Please come back home."

WHAT ONCE WAS HIDDEN

Thank you God for chasing me
It's for my heart that you have fought
I will not run away but run to you
Because I just wanna be caught.

I will not run away but run to you
Because I just wanna be caught.

In the Midst of Chaos

Jesus is amazing. I just love reading about his life here on earth. He was so calm in the midst of chaos. Just read Mark 5:21–43.

I always thought that there had to be order for anything to be truly successful. One of my favorite experiences that helped debunk this thinking was during a ministry trip to the Netherlands. We had a team of students and leaders who went into the schools to teach about "the life of an American student," which happened to include our faith stories.

One of our events was an invite to a Friday night gathering where we hoped and prayed for connection with the students so God could move in and do what he does best—speak hope into hearts and lives. What happened this night opened my eyes to see just how God works in the midst of chaos.

Our turnout for this event was massive. It was wall-to-wall people, loud and noisy and lots of crazy fun going on. I couldn't imagine that anything of any significance could actually transpire in that atmosphere. I felt discouraged. That's when God pointed me in the direction of a young man named Rakesh. I had spent some time talking with Rakesh during school hours. He was a quiet and gentle boy from a Hindu home. And he was a curious boy. I wondered how he was processing all that he was hearing about our God being the one true God when he lived in a home that had multiple gods being worshipped.

Rakesh showed up to our after school event. I could've easily missed him because the crowd was overwhelming. But God had other plans. At one point, I needed a break from the chaos so I stepped out of the gym area to get a drink of water. I looked to my right, and sitting on the steps in the partial dark was Rakesh. I went over to him and sat down, asking him if he was okay.

He began to tell me that he wanted to know more about this God we had been talking about. He wanted to know how he could have a future in the heaven we talked about. He said that his mother and father had all these god statues all over the house, but he didn't believe in them anymore. He didn't want to worship them, but he was afraid that his family would disown him.

In that moment, I knew without a shadow of a doubt that God was wooing Rakesh to himself and he was going to do his mighty work in the midst of all this chaos. At the very moment when I asked Rakesh if he would like to go somewhere a bit more quiet, my husband "happened" to walk out where we were sitting. So the three of us went to a quiet room and we shared the full gospel with Rakesh. I watched the face of this boy transform before my eyes. He lit up as he began to understand that God's love and forgiveness was available to him as well. I wish I could have taken a picture of his face. The presence of the Lord calling him was so tangible.

Rakesh made a decision that night in a quiet room. God pushed the noise and distractions to the outskirts of this room so that Rakesh could step into a relationship with him. The tears began to flow. He chose God over his family. He chose God over "many gods." He was the bravest young man I've ever met.

I often think of Rakesh. I received a letter from him months after we met. He said that he found a church that teaches about Jesus, that he got "dipped" (baptized) and felt like a new person. His mother and sister were attending with him and no longer believe in many gods. One day, I will be face-to-face with Rakesh when we both step into the beautiful chaos of heaven welcoming home its own.

Left in the Dark

When I was in kindergarten, we always held a concert for the entire elementary school at the end of the school year. It was a long evening for anyone to sit through, especially kindergarteners, so the teachers came up with an idea. We would go onstage and perform first and then we would be taken back to our perspective rooms where pieces of carpet, blankets, and pillows would await us in a dark room. We were told to "rest" until our parent(s) came to collect us after the whole concert was over.

I'm not really sure who came up with that idea, but they certainly didn't think it through from a kindergartener's perspective. Sure, this was a familiar room that we spent half days in all week long, but we knew these rooms in the daylight, not at night. Nothing looked familiar. Every shadow moved on its own, and every sound seemed like someone was trying to sneak into our room.

I can clearly remember lying on my carpet, wondering if my dad and grandpa, who brought me, would forget me. As the concert came to an end, parents began to show up to collect their child. One after another disappeared from my room. The line of parents was thinning, and I was slowly becoming part of a shrinking number of children. At some point, I truly believed I had been forgotten. I began to cry as the fear of being left in that building all night began to consume me. As one kind mother picked up her child, she saw my distress and asked me what was wrong. I began to tell her my fear, and just as I started, I looked up, and there was the familiar faces of my father and grandfather, the last two people in the line!

The fear of being forgotten is not just for the young of mind. Many of us have become fearful adults and have wondered if our Heavenly Father has forgotten us. We struggle with life, often alone and feeling lonely in our struggle, and we wonder if God has flicked us off the end of his finger and left us to deal with our fears.

But, unlike my father and grandfather that night, God is not the last in line to reach us. He is not playing hide-and-seek and peeking around the corner at the eleventh hour. We are always in his view.

> "Can a mother forget the baby at her breast and have no compassion on the child she has borne? Though she may forget, *I will never forget you*! See, I have carved you on the palms of my hands." Isaiah 49:15–16

The next time you think you are coming up empty-handed and feeling forgotten, just turn your hands over, look at them, and then think about Jesus doing the same exact thing. Imagine what he sees when he looks at his pierced hands. He sees *you*. Always.

Lighten Up

I think every husband who ever tries to surprise his wife with romance should get kudos for the effort, even if it doesn't go quite the way he wanted.

Since I am the one who would typically orchestrate "mood setting," you can imagine my surprise when I walked into my room and my hubby had made a valiant attempt to bathe our room in candlelight. He knows how much I love candles.

When I saw what he had done, I was surprised that he didn't look so happy. He was trying so hard to have this surprise ready and he said he was really frustrated when one of my candles just wouldn't light.

When I asked which candle, he said, "The white one on the wood-burning stove. I tried and tried but it just wouldn't light, so I almost gave up."

I tried to contain my laugh. "Tom, that's my *fake* candle!" It runs on batteries!"

We both just started laughing.

I wonder if John the Baptist could relate to this scenario. When John came on the scene, many of the Jewish religious leaders came to him asking him who he was. "Are *you* the Messiah? Are *you* the Prophet? Are *you* the Light of the world?"

No, I am not. I am just a witness. I'm not the real deal. The *real* Light is coming! I'm just showing you the way!

John 1:8–9 says, he (John) was not the light; he came only as a witness to the light. The *true* Light was coming into the world.

The Pharisees were so caught up in who John was and what his purpose was that they missed the coming of the Messiah.

"I baptize with water," said John, "but among you stands One you do not know."

Jesus said, "I am the light of the world. Whoever follows me will never walk in darkness, but will have the light of life" (John 8:12).

Sometimes, we miss the real deal because we are trying so hard to make something (or someone) light up our world. Find Jesus. There is no match.

Master Gardening

I have been in the presence of a dying woman during her last day on earth. I didn't know it at the time. I just knew she didn't have much time left.

Her name was Whitney. I had visited her on other occasions during her declining health, but this time brought a sense of urgency. So I went.

The moment I walked into her room and saw her, I knew I was breathing the same air as a woman who was taking her last earthly breaths. What do you do in that moment, especially when the dying person can no longer speak? I felt moved to speak on her behalf. I began to pray and sing.

It was just Whitney, me, and Jesus in that room. I sensed his presence, and it brought me a great deal of peace in the face of inevitable death.

I'm not a great singer, but songs started pouring out of me: "Amazing Grace," "I Love You, Lord," "Silent Night," "Step by Step (I Will Follow You All of My Days)," and "I Can Only Imagine." But when I began to sing "Open My Eyes, Lord," something happened. Up to this point, I wondered if she could hear me and understand the words I was singing. But when I got to the line that says, "I want to see Jesus, to reach out and touch him...," she smiled a faint smile, squeezed my hand several times, and a single tear streamed down her face.

There were so many moments I wished she could open her eyes, speak to me what she was feeling and thinking, but it was not to be. Her next words most likely were spoken while breathing celestial air and seeing Jesus face-to-face.

I wasn't afraid of facing death. I didn't feel afraid of speaking about what is to come to Whitney...our hope for a future without pain or suffering, no longer a body decaying and broken. Instead, I reminded her that it won't be long now before she would run on streets of gold and be made whole again.

In this life, Whitney was a master gardener. I'll just bet she is gardening for the Master now!

He makes everything new.

He makes everything whole.

He makes hope come alive again.

And I'll bet heaven's gardens never looked better.

Masterpiece

Masterpiece—*noun*
- a work of outstanding artistry, skill, or workmanship.

When you think of a masterpiece, what comes to mind? The *Mona Lisa* or *The Last Supper* by Leonardo da Vinci? *The Creation of Adam*, the statue of David, or *Pieta* by Michelangelo? *The Starry Night* by Vincent Van Gogh? Maybe your masterpiece is more personal like a lovely piece of artwork on your refrigerator by one of your children or grandkids. Our world is filled with the creative geniuses of artists around the world.

Question for you...did it enter your mind that *you* are a masterpiece? Not because I say that you are. You are a masterpiece because the Great I Am says you are.

> "For we are God's *masterpiece*, created in Christ Jesus to do good works, which God prepared in advance for us to do" (Eph. 2:10).

Each one of us had this moment when God decided who we would be. I wonder what God was thinking and feeling when he knit me together in my mother's womb. What was it like to be intimately involved in creating each one of us? Did he turn to Jesus and the Holy Spirit and say with delight, "Let's begin"?

Psalm 139:13 says, "You created my inmost being; you knit me together in my mother's womb." What exactly does it look like for the Creator to knit?

How did he decide the intimate details that make up me? Who decided that I would have skin that tans a golden brown, blue eyes, and long legs? Who decided that I would have an analytical spirit, softness for the elderly, and a creative gene that needs an avenue to express itself?

Have you ever wondered what the Creator thought when knitting *you* together? Here's the cool thing. You have a depth of personality, emotions, feelings, and thoughts that are uniquely you because you were created by a unique God. There is not one inch of you, head to toe, inside and out, that God did not intend to be a part of who you are. And there are no copycats. You are an original. There will never be another you. You are rare.

People come from all over the world to see some of the greatest masterpieces, like the ones mentioned above. Wouldn't it be cool if each one of us displayed our lives as a living masterpiece for the world to see? God's precious works of art, on display for all to see.

One Blood

Just the word blood can cause some to faint. Then there are those who have careers that require you to face bloody, life-threatening moments every day. I salute you. Even though I am in neither of these categories, the impact of seeing blood in a surprising situation took me off guard one time with my dad.

At seventy-nine years of age, my dad was not a physically stable man, but he still loved to cook. He was the king of making soups. One evening, he went out to his garage refrigerator and grabbed a very large kettle of soup to bring indoors for dinner. He and the soup never made it.

He lost his balance on the steps, falling backward, hitting his head on the concrete floor in the garage. He was able to alert my mom, who called for help. By the time my husband and I arrived, my brother was already there.

One thing you need to know is that my dad took blood thinners. He also had fallen in a way that his legs were elevated on the stairs, causing all the blood to rush to his head.

So when I walked into the garage, my first view of him was lying in a pool of blood. I watched for movement. Was he alive? That's when I heard his voice talking to my brother.

I turned around, ran back to my husband, and said, "There is so much blood!"

Once he was in the hospital, they were able to treat him and get the bleeding under control.

I wonder how many onlookers at the time of the Crucifixion wanted to "stop the bleeding." How many people said, "There is so much blood!" But we all know it was necessary! We *needed* that blood to flow so that *we* could have continued life. Eternal life.

My son shared a song with me from a movie I've never seen, but I love the song. It reminded me so much of Jesus and his sacrifice.

The song is called "One Blood." It talks about there being only one blood that matters and a river that ran red with shame.

How many times do we personally feel shame and need to run to the "River of Life," looking for the cleansing blood of Christ and its rich provisions?

It talks about a world where danger and war no longer exist (aka heaven?)

And it talks about a person taking another's suffering if it would do any good. The suffering of Christ *did* do more than good. It redeemed us for *all* eternity.

And when the bleeding of the Savior stopped, the healing began.

Thank you, Jesus, for enduring the bloody Cross.

Parades and Princesses

Does every little girl dream of going to Disney and hanging out with all the princesses? Even better, do they wish to *be* one of the princesses?

My granddaughter Chloie went to Disney and she could not wait to meet one particular character. You might think it was one of the elegantly dressed princesses we all know like Cinderella or Belle. But she had her heart set on someone a bit more adventurous…Mulan.

As part of her package, she was taken to a meal with all the female Disney characters. At this event, the guests were invited to be a part of a parade led by the characters.

As most parents do, cameras were out to capture the moment. Without hesitation, Chloie gathered with all the characters where they would enter the room and begin the parade.

Cue the music.

Begin videotaping.

Start the procession.

Oh my, guess who appears in the entrance? Chloie had wiggled her way into the hand and heart of Mulan, and they were leading the whole parade! My eyes swelled with tears as she came around the corner, weaving her way through the crowds, waving a royal princess wave. It just melted my heart.

Why did this touch me so deeply? I think it spoke to the reality deep down in all of us who long to be seen as a princess. Not only do we want to be valued, but we want to lead in this parade of life with dignity and grace, with our hero by our side.

Take Jesus' hand. Wave at the crowds and give them your best princess smile. His sacrifice has elevated you to the front of the parade!

Psalm 16:8 states, "I keep my eyes always on the Lord. With him at my right hand, I shall not be shaken."

Motherhood through the Ages

When my mother turned seventy-six, I felt something sentimental. We had been through so much together as mother and daughter. There have been so many stages.

I remember being "mommy's little helper." I loved learning how to be a homemaker. She taught me the value of being organized, how to make a house a home, and she was by my side when I baked my first cake.

Six years after I was born, my sister was born. My mom taught me how to care for a baby. I quickly embraced being a "second mother" to my baby sister, and my love for babies grew. I knew then that my dream was to be a mother.

As the years passed and I moved into adolescence, I became self-absorbed. Boys, not baking, called for my attention. Appearance became more important than character, and that set me on a collision course of headbutting and the infamous withdraw from my mother.

But mothers fight. And they protect. My mother fought for my integrity, my purity, my honor, and my character. She entered the relational war, and many times she did it alone. It began those tumultuous years when you have one foot in the "love camp" and one foot in the "hate camp." As I look back, I realize that my mom had *both* feet firmly planted in the love camp and, with outstretched arms, she was desperately reaching into the hate camp to draw me back. She was my rescuer.

It was a bloody battle. I thought I was the one with all the scars and wounds to prove it. But now I know I was more unscathed than my mother. I was deep in the hate camp, but *she*, she was stretched to the maximum to reach me and keep both feet firmly planted in the love camp. I didn't know it then, choosing not to see, but I know it now. Boy, do I know it.

For time pressed forward and with it came the phase of mother-daughter as mother to mother. That one act of holding your own child in your arms for the first time ignites a flashback, a time machine traveling back if you will, and you finally get it. You finally understand your mother. You understand the fierceness of that "overprotective" mother, that "meddling, persistent" mother, that woman who had made it her mission to come between you and all the foolish frenzies of a lovestruck teenage girl.

And now you *need* her.
You need her wisdom.
You need her support.
You need her encouragement.
You need her unconditional love.

And you realize in that moment of time that your mother is your biggest fan! She has been cheering for you at every stage of your life.

The years roll by and your mother becomes a great-grandmother and you become a grandmother.

And the great-grandmother becomes childlike and the daughter becomes motherlike.

My mother now has dementia, and even though she still knows me, I pray that all those years she loved with selfless love I can now return.

And the cycle begins all over again.

No Hiding Place

The day begins as all days do,
The window light comes shining through.
I hardly take the time to hear
And yet I sense his presence near.

But life, it calls me to be full
I search for pleasures, never dull
And still I feel the ache inside
Yet from this God, I choose to hide.

I heard his voice not long ago
And I vowed to always go
Where his voice was calling me
Because his death had set me free.

And then somehow I lost my way
And chose to keep my God at bay
Embracing life, I chose my sin
And kept my God from ent'ring in.

And now this mother aches for you
My precious ones, I'll pray you through
You can hide or you can run
It matters not when day is done
For this is not our real home
And God is still upon his throne.

Pinball Wizardry

I love pinball machines. I might be dating myself with that statement, but I do. I love the challenge, the sights and sounds, and the speed at which you have to play the game. I love being a maniac with the flippers and the rapid fire of the balls coming at you in all different directions. But when the quarters run out, I walk away from the chaos under the glass and go on my way.

Sometimes life feels like a never-ending pinball machine.

Once the lever is pulled (waking to a new day), the pinballs (thoughts, challenges) start flying all over the place, with some ricocheting, appearing over and over again. The flashing lights and bells remind me of the pulls of life trying to get my attention and telling me to stay in the game, to rack up the points for the win. But with most pinball games, I usually fall short of winning the grand prize. I invest and invest and come up short of the win.

Life *without* God is much the same way. It sends us constant messages that we can win if we try harder, so we pour more and more into the "game" until we walk away defeated.

But life *with* God adds its purpose, its direction, the manual for enjoying the game. It makes the most difficult situations bearable. It unleashes us to live fully, endure obstacles, and rise to the challenges.

Jesus said, "I have told you these things *so that* in me you may have peace. In this world you will have trouble but take heart! I have overcome the world!" (John 16:33).

Jesus. The original pinball wizard. He doesn't get the grand prize. He *is* the grand prize!

Shattered Security

I was a city girl during the days of my youth. Our family experienced many memories in the city of Detroit. Our neighborhood was full of people doing what we were doing: surviving, making ends meet, and experiencing the occasional sights and sounds that come with city life.

One such night is burned into my memory. My whole family had already settled into bed. I had my own room. It was a small room and the bed was placed directly underneath a window. It wasn't something I ever felt comfortable with, but it had to be so. As we all began our deeper sleeps and the only sounds of the night were the crickets, we were jarred awake by the sound of smashing glass. It sounded like what I would imagine if a bullet had been shot through a window.

Fear crept in and I lay in my bed, paralyzed. The only thing I could think of was, "Where is my dad?" My dad was a largely built strong man. If there was trouble and he was near, I knew I was safe. As I settled into this thought, I could hear my dad and my brother whispering.

My brother said, "I'm scared, Dad!" (Good, someone said what my fear wouldn't let me say.)

I anticipated my dad calming our fears. That's when I looked to the left and saw my father in the hallway outside my bedroom door, crawling on all fours, saying, "I'm scared too."

In that moment, all my security and safety in my father perished. He was admitting a weakness in himself that never dawned on me. My father could be afraid. He could be insecure.

I lay in bed with this newfound reality swirling around in my head as he crawled through the rest of the house, looking for the culprit of the disturbance. We ended up going back to sleep with no answers, no fear relieved, no comfort or security.

Years later, I met and began a relationship with my Heavenly Father. When I came to an understanding of who God is and what he offers, I found a security that is based in reality. I found a father who can speak into my fears and say, "Do not be afraid. I am with you always, even to the end of the age."

He is our *only* unchanging security.

"I, the Lord, do not change" (Mal. 3:6).

He is our *only* true source of comfort and caretaker of our fears.

"Praise be to the God and Father of our Lord Jesus Christ, the Father of compassion and the God of all comfort" (2 Cor. 1:3).

"Never will I leave you; never will I forsake you. So we say with confidence, 'the Lord is my helper, I will not be afraid. What can man do to me?'" (Heb. 13:5–6)

He knows our future and secures it.

"I know the plans I have for you, declares the Lord, plans to prosper you and not to harm you, plans to give you hope and a future" (Jer. 29:11).

As Paul Harvey would often say, "Now, for the rest of the story…"

The next morning, when we were getting ready for school, we had a great laugh and a deep sense of relief. My dad, who had left for work earlier, discovered the source of the shattered noise from the night before. A can of crescent dough had exploded in the refrigerator, hitting a glass bottle of ketchup, shattering it to pieces. In his creative way, my dad shaped the dough into a little dough boy and left the message:

> "Sorry if I disturbed your sleep last night,
> but I guess I just blew my top."
> —The Poppin' Dough Boy

It's funny what God will use to strip away false security so he can show us where our true security lies.

In what are you placing your security? Are you completely certain that your source of security can deliver 100 percent of the time?

Rollercoaster

I am the God of the mountain
But also the valley below
If you will let me, I'll show up
In your moments of highs and lows.

I am the God of your triumphs
But stay when your failures abound
I'm here on the rollercoaster
For all of your ups and downs.

Give me your burdens and troubles
Let me take care of your sin.
Just trust me for the journey
Find me and new life begins.

The world is full of false pleasure
Promising thrills that will last
I offer the ride of a lifetime
That began with the Cross of the past.

Come, follow me for adventures
Leave all your troubles behind
Come on the ride of a lifetime
Because I'm not the leaving kind.

                                        - God

Smoke Screens

In the movie *The Mask of Zorro*, we are invited into a world of injustice where the dons of California are building their wealth on the backs of the poor and helpless. A new "Zorro" has been trained by an older Zorro for the purpose of helping these oppressed people. One of the dons has "employed" the unfortunate as prisoners to mine for gold.

Zorro, who learns the ways of a gentleman so he can infuse himself into the world of the dons, becomes privy to his secret mine. He goes back to the older Zorro and reveals the injustice he has seen. Then, a plan is put into action.

Both Zorros, along with Helena, the daughter of the eldest Zorro, go to the people to help free them. When they get to the mining site, all the people have been caged like animals and dynamite lines have been strung to their soon-to-be tombs.

Zorro and Helena begin running from cage to cage to shoot the locks off. They are racing against time as the dynamite line is burning closer and closer. All of a sudden, a huge explosion takes place and the audience sees nothing but a screen of smoke.

In that minute, we are all left wondering, "Did the heroes of the story just die giving his and her life?" Did they just fail in their heroic effort to bring victory to the people? We wait…we wait, the smoke clears and, in slow motion, we see the faint figures of the heroes break through the smoke surrounded by the people they came to rescue.

There is a verse in Ephesians 6:13 that says, "Therefore, put on the full armor of God, so that when the day of evil comes, you may be able to stand your ground, and after you have done everything, to stand."

I have read this verse so many times and focused completely on the full armor of God part. Then God removed the "smoke screen" for me and the words *to stand* jumped out at me.

Even though we are called to "fight the good fight" and more than often we might come out of the battle limping, beat up, and bruised, we are called to stand! To be victorious! Why? Because it's what the armor of God does! It equips us for the battle!

Swords up, fellow soldiers!

Talk Me out of It!

Most, if not all of us, have seen *The Wizard of Oz*. Dorothy has developed this friendship with three unlikely characters: the Scarecrow, the Tin Man, and the Cowardly Lion. She is on a journey to Emerald City to meet the Wizard of Oz and ask him to send her back home to Kansas. Little does each of these characters know that they are also on a journey in search of a brain, a heart, and courage.

Dorothy is captured by the Wicked Witch of the West and held captive in her castle. Each of her new friends can't bear what she is facing, so they come together with a plan for her rescue. We open up on a scene where they are climbing up a stony wall that surrounds the castle, looking for a way to penetrate the castle and rescue Dorothy.

Let's eavesdrop on their conversation.

The Scarecrow and Tin Man tell the Cowardly Lion that he is going to lead them to Dorothy. At first he resists. After all, he *is* on a journey looking for courage. But then he thinks of Dorothy being locked up in that evil castle, and with a new strength he says, "I'll do it for Dorothy. I just have one thing I want you to do for me."

"What's that?"

"Talk me out of it!"

Have you ever been asked by God to do something that you just didn't confidently feel that you could do? I have, many times. And it seems that is his pattern. Looking back into the Scripture, I see that he did this over and over. And it often was not a pretty picture.

Abraham led God's people to the land flowing with milk and honey, but he didn't get to enter it with them. Moses had to return time and time again and face the rejection of the Pharaoh when he asked him to "Let God's people go." Joseph had to endure false accusation and being thrown into prison. And then there is Jesus…well, what he endured was so unbearable, but so necessary.

God's plan always has people "going." He sends people to fulfill his plan. Just read Psalm 105. He is still asking us to do the same.

Recently, he asked me to go to a place that I have no desire to visit: Las Vegas. There is nothing about Las Vegas that excites me or intrigues me, except for one thing: a person, my oldest son.

My relationship with my oldest son has been a challenge. We've had our share of ups and downs, hard knocks, and estrangement from one another. So you can imagine my resistance when I heard God whisper, "Go. I want you to go to your son." And I felt like he wanted me to take only two things with me: his love and his promise. "If God is for us, who can be against us?" (Rom 8:31).

I felt just like the Cowardly Lion. I wanted my friends to talk me out of it. It felt too scary and too uncertain to imagine being face-to-face with my son. But I did it because I love my son, and so does God.

I felt God going before me and with me. And just like the Cowardly Lion, I felt the support of my friends, who came with me "in prayer." I wasn't being asked to do this alone.

So if you ever feel like your feet are planted in cement when God asks you to go, believe him for the outcome. It will play out exactly as he has already seen. Take courage with you. It's in you already, just like the Cowardly Lion discovered.

Shackled

You see me on my knees, head bowed, hands turned up.

You see worship. You wait for me to lift my hands in praise.
But I stay bowed to the ground, frozen in shame.

I see what you don't see…

I see the chains that shackle me to my shame and guilt.
I *can't* lift my hands in praise.
It would reveal that I am in shackles and then you would
Really know me.

You would know that I am not free…
…nor in control.
You would know I am afraid,
…feeling worthless.
You would see that I am condemned.

"Let there be no condemnation for those who are in Christ Jesus."

Let your shackles fall to the ground.
Reach for the key to unlock your chains.
Reach for the Cross.

That Four-Letter Word

There are many four-letter words that are unpleasant to hear. They just make us cringe. I am adding a new one. This four-letter word seems to bring out the worst in me. Maybe it does you as well, especially if it's being spoken straight from the mouth of God.

W-A-I-T.

I don't know about you, but when my desire for something is so strong, this one word can send me into a tailspin. Intellectually, I know the Lord has reasons beyond my understanding when he asks me to wait. But my longing stirs sometimes and the next thing I know, my patience wanes and I have wiggled myself right into the driver's seat.

I confess that I often need to just "pull the car over," put it in park, and get back in the passenger seat where I belong. Sometimes, I think God needs my help getting out of a detour so we can get to my desired destination through the fastest route.

My husband and I took my parents on a driving trip for their fiftieth anniversary. We had it all mapped out, but my dad is infamous for finding "the back roads." Toward the end of our trip, he was trying to convince my husband to take a detour from the expressway. It would take us out of our way, and we just wanted to get to our next destination. But he insisted and we relented. I'm glad that we did. We ended up traveling along a beautiful river with scenery that was worth every extra second.

Have you ever wondered what you might have missed if God took you straight through certain travels of life? He has a way of showing us so many things we would have otherwise missed if he didn't keep us "wandering in the desert."

Maybe "wait" is not such a bad word. If we rush, we miss out on the journey. And isn't that all life is, one great, big adventurous journey?

Have you ever thought about what it's like for God to wait? He has infinite power and could act anytime he so chooses in any way he so chooses, but he *chooses* the act of waiting because of his immense love for us and his deep knowledge of what we truly need.

I think of the times my kids asked for something and pleaded their case for why they needed it immediately. Sometimes I would say yes immediately, other times I would hold off knowing there was a better choice ahead. That wasn't always pretty, but one thing I learned for certain is that there was always a greater joy when something was waited for.

Maybe you are waiting for God to strengthen your marriage.

Maybe you are waiting for a prodigal child to return.

Maybe you are waiting for financial relief.

Maybe you are waiting on health issues to be resolved.

We all have stuff, right?

I am slowly learning to be okay in the waiting.

I am learning to not be a bratty, whiny kid when I ask God for something and he says, "You'll have to wait."

I just have to look over and see who is in the driver's seat.

I am learning that he already studied the "map" and my life is going exactly in the direction he intended all along.

Stay Alive!

"You will seek me and find me when you seek me with all your heart. I will be found by you," declares the Lord, "and I will bring you back from captivity" (Jer. 29:13–14).

In the movie, *The Last of the Mohicans*, Daniel Day Lewis plays the character Natty. He is a Mohican Indian that falls in love with an American woman, Cora. For the greater good, Natty has to leave Cora behind and flee from a ruthless Indian tribe. As this enemy is hot on their trail, Natty says to Cora, "Just stay alive! I *will* find you!"

She becomes his object of great affection, and he promises to return and rescue her. He will stop at nothing to be with her again. With that promise, Cora does what she has to do to stay alive. He becomes the focus in her head and heart that keeps her alive.

It's such a powerful scene. Even though he has to leave her behind to fight the enemy on her own, he gives her hope of his return. And it motivates her to be all that she can be until he comes to seek her out again.

This is such a vivid picture of the hope and promise of the Crucifixion. Even though the event was surrounded by confusion, danger, and uncertainty, Jesus made it very clear that temporarily leaving us through his death was necessary for him to be able to fulfill his promise to return for us.

"I *will* come back and take you to be with me that you may also be with me" (John 14:3).

Just stay alive, he implores. Keep your heart and hope alive!

Shoulders

What's the big deal about shoulders? They can be kind of knobby, broad, or a hanging post for a purse. But have you ever thought of their location on the body? They are like sentinels on either side of one of our most precious organs—the heart.

I don't think that's a coincidence. How often have we been drawn close to another person, between their shoulders, and embraced close to their heart? How lovely we feel when someone stretches their arms wide to welcome us into a warm hug. And for lovers, how often has the rapid heartbeat felt in an embrace spoke volumes to us about what the other person is feeling?

It's no wonder that Deuteronomy 33:12 says, "And the one (that's you and me) that the Lord loves rests between his shoulders."

It reminds me of this image. I envision that woman is me. Can you see yourself? Just close your eyes and picture yourself in the embrace of your perfect and holy Savior.

Think about the joy he must feel when one of his redeemed comes and enjoys his love, falling into his arms of safety. We can delight in knowing that Jesus is our constant friend and we have an intimacy of soul with him that is matchless.

If you know Jesus intimately as Savior, you can be certain that one day you will cry tears of joy when it is your restored body resting between his shoulders, heart-to-heart and face-to-face with Love.

The Blind Babysitter

My family has lifelong friends who have raised a blind daughter. She is an incredibly independent woman. Her tenacity to not be defined by her blindness has always inspired me. One of the things that she is deeply drawn to is babies and children. Because of this, we trusted her to babysit our young boys. We didn't worry when she cared for them because her senses were beyond amazing, and it helped that our boys just loved her.

Our youngest son will tell the story of climbing up on the counter once to grab something out of the cupboard and Terri immediately said, "Bryan, get off that counter!" He said he wondered how she knew when she couldn't see!

Another time, she made them popcorn and one of the boys accidentally spilled the bowl. When we got home, she was profusely apologetic, saying she tried to pick up the spilled popcorn and hoped she got it all. I looked around and didn't see one single kernel of corn! She was just that efficient!

I often think of Terri when I think of God's redeeming love. I wonder what it will be like for her when God restores her one day and she "sees" for the first time.

There was a blind man who encountered Jesus in the Bible. After restoring his sight, Jesus asks him, "Do you believe in the Son of Man?" "Who is he, sir?" the man asked. "Tell me so that I may believe in him." Jesus said, "You have now seen him; in fact, he is the one speaking with you." Then the man said, "Lord, I believe" and he worshipped him.

What a spiritual awakening! I wonder what it was like for that man to look into the eyes of Jesus after receiving physical sight for the first time and to be told, "You are looking at the Son of Man!"

What did he see in Jesus' eyes, hear in his voice, feel in his gentle touch as he restored his sight?

This is the kind of Savior we serve! He restores us physically, emotionally, and spiritually, and he does it with great delight!

I hope I am standing somewhere near Jesus when Terri sees for the first time. What a sight that will be to see!

The Chain-Link Fence

I met two women who were residing in a shelter for women. They had been through a lifestyle that I can only imagine. The streets were their place of employment and they had faced the beatings of many of their clients. They had been rescued out of prostitution and drug addiction and brought to the shelter with hope for a new life.

I became particularly connected to these two women. Somehow, they came to trust me as a friend. I didn't take that lightly as I'm sure their trust had been abused and misused in countless ways. I wasn't sure what it was that they were drawn to, but I was soon to find out.

We spent days and evenings together, talking and learning about each other. I learned that one of them had lost a child from her choices. I learned that every time they were given free time, they battled just walking down a street and facing the pull to find drugs. I learned that they loved Jesus in spite of their hard lives. I learned that they wanted freedom in Christ, freedom from the strongholds that had brought them to the shelter. I learned that they were not very different from me in their longings and desires.

I came to love them. I didn't want our time together to end, but I knew it would. After a week, our team was loading up the vans to head home. I didn't want to leave until I said goodbye to these two women. They were not at the shelter that morning because they had a program they were attending. They were returning at any moment. Everything in me begged for more time until they returned. I just couldn't leave.

Our vans were parked on the other side of a chain-linked fence that surrounded the "playground" of the shelter. I kept looking back at the doors of the shelter as we loaded up the last of the suitcases and team. That's when I heard it, the bus pulling in the shelter and the cries of my name. I turned and saw these two women running across the playground, calling out my name, tears streaming down their faces. Our driver was ready to head out, but I ran up to the fence where they were. I hated that the fence was between us. I needed to wrap my arms around them as much as they needed to wrap theirs around me. We extended our fingers through the fence, gripping each other's fingers, crying as we connected one last time.

And in that moment, one of them said these words to me that I will never forget. She looked at me through tears and said, "I knew that I could trust you because, from the first time I met you, I saw the love of Jesus in your eyes."

In all my years of being a Christian, I had never heard those words from another person. They were words that I tucked deep into my soul because it was a reminder to me of what *all* Christians are meant to be. We are not to be seen. We are to be a reflection of Jesus! We are to simply be vessels that his love shines through. There was absolutely nothing about my love that could save those women, but there is *everything* about the love of Jesus that could offer them hope. He broke the barrier of every chain-linked fence, every barrier, and every stronghold, and stepped into our world, our hearts, and our lives.

Embrace him and you will never, ever be the same.

The Eyes of a Child

Have you ever had a time when God disrupts your agenda for a simple teaching moment? This happened to me while I was serving at a center for the homeless. I had the privilege of working in the kitchen and my duties were laid out for me. Prep the food. Check. Fill the bins with napkins and plasticware. Check. Wash off the tables in the dining hall. Check. Everything was going according to plan so we could feed lunch to the people of the streets.

I suppose each of us has an idea of what a homeless person looks like. Movies have stereotyped them as a man with bad teeth and a scrawny beard or woman with a filthy overcoat and wiry, unkempt hair. We believe these are the down-on-their-luck of society who have made bad choices and ended up in bad places.

As these folks were ushered into the dining area, I was not prepared for the three generations of family that came through the door. A grandfather, his adult son, and a grandchild came in and took a seat at a table. The child was young enough that he required a high chair. Once they were seated, I made my way over to their table. Something about this child drew my heart to him. I noticed three things about him.

His grandfather tenderly cared for him.
His face was covered in filthy dirt.
He had beautiful blue eyes.

I bent down to his level to say hello. His face registered me as a complete stranger. But to me, he registered as a connection. Maybe it's because I had my own blue-eyed little boys, but I sensed a connection to this child.

I went to the kitchen and grabbed the only dishcloth I could find. I wet it with warm water and headed back to this little boy. As I bent down and started washing his face, it was in that moment that

I realized the room became eerily still. All eyes were watching this simple act of kindness. To me, it felt like the common sense thing to do ("did you wash up before dinner?"), but to the homeless, it apparently spoke volumes. These were people of the streets who are often marginalized, forgotten, or avoided. Their very exteriors make us uncomfortable.

As I finished washing this child's face, I noticed the grandfather had tears going down his face. He looked at me and said, "Why would you do this for us?"

It was such a simple question but was packed with so much emotion. I simply said, "Because everyone deserves to be loved."

That night, I went to my warm room with my soft bed and wondered about that child. Homelessness had a new face and I didn't like it. I didn't like what it revealed in me. I thought God had called me to serve in the city because I was capable. What I learned is that God called me to the city to show me how incapable I am. I had little to offer this child, but God showed me he had what each homeless person needs…a loving touch to restore their dignity and their hope.

The words of the grandfather helped me to see that. He didn't understand why I would kneel before his grandson and care for him. He didn't believe they deserved it.

It's amazing how our station in life can develop the idea that we are above others. The chase after wealth and status can often leave us forgetting our roots.

Ecclesiastes 3:20 says, "All go to the same place; *all come from dust* and to dust all return."

Genesis 2:7 says, "Then the Lord God formed a man from the *dust of the ground* and breathed into his nostrils the breath of life."

I am thankful that God put me face-to-face with the homeless, the underprivileged. Why? Because I saw *my* reflection in their eyes. It reminded me that I was homeless before being adopted into the family of God. I was underprivileged until God gave me *his* royal position and standing. I couldn't even muster up a breath without him breathing life into me.

Our "dirtyness" and "sickness" became his through his sacrifice. He touched lepers and they were healed. He brought life back to a daughter of a high-positioned centurion. He does not separate the wealthy from the poor, the learned from the unlearned, the healthy from the sick. At the foot of the Cross, each of us comes poverty-stricken. At the foot of the Cross, we are *all* broken and in need of his grace. No one is exempt. No one.

Standing the Test of Time

When I was just a toddler, my parents bought a blonde wood dresser that held all my little girl clothes. Even though it is now stained a darker color and has upgraded knobs, it's amazing to me that a piece of furniture could last in *any* child's room for more than a few years. This dresser has survived me, two sons and several grandchildren!

It's remarkable to me that, in a day and age where we go through everything from the latest sports shoes to the most updated version of cell phones at lightning speed, I still have this piece of furniture. I know it's just a dresser, but it has sentimental value to me. It's connected to my childhood. And when it would have been cool to upgrade to the latest trend in furnishings, I couldn't part with that dresser. It's just…well…a part of me.

My Creator God once spoke to his beloved children and said to them, "I have loved you with an everlasting love."

In a time when we tire easily and quickly of things, situations, and even people, it's good to know that we have a Father who delights in standing the test of time with his love for us. He could no more toss us aside than I could let that dresser be sent to the junkyard.

He sees great value in you and me. And like my dresser, he has been tenacious in "refurbishing" us. We might have a few dents and scratches, but he sees our value as his children.

It's comforting to know that when God uses words like everlasting and eternal, he doesn't use them lightly. He uses them to speak truth about his character. His love is endless, boundless…

I know there will come a day when this dresser will no longer have sentimental value to anyone and it will be thrown to the curb for garbage day, but until then, it serves as a great reminder of things that stand the test of time.

The Great Lye

You may have caught my title and thought, "Oops, a misspelling." It's not. It's intentional. Let me tell you a story that to this day reveals my rebellious spirit.

My husband and I were visiting an Amish community and the place we were staying offered guided tours of Amish life. They had several small buildings that highlighted different activities from their lives. I am fascinated by the Amish and their simple ways, so off to the tour we went.

A group of us gathered with the guide. I had my camera with me, as photography is a great love of mine. It became apparent from the get-go that the tour was going to move slower than we had anticipated and I was itching to explore and take some photos. So I pulled my hubby quietly away from the tour and began looking around.

The first building we came to had no door on it, so I peeked inside. I saw these layered trays filled with a creamy, buttery-looking substance. "Ooh," I thought, "homemade creamy butter!" I headed into the small space, thinking, "Just a taste won't hurt anything!" Of course, my husband is advising against it. Here is where my rebellious spirit came out. I said, "I'm just going to dip my pinky in it and taste it," so I did. Immediately, I realized that something wasn't right. It wasn't butter at all.

We decided to round the corner of the building and rejoin the tour guide. He was in the middle of explaining to the group how to make lye soap. As he described all the ingredients that went into it, he said, "And certainly no one would ever intentionally get this in their eyes or ingest it because it would burn them."

From my side, I heard the soft voice of my husband say, "Except for my wife!" Now at this point, the end of my tongue is on fire! I connect the dots and realize that what appeared to be rich, creamy butter was actually trays of lye soap!

It took almost a week for my tongue to heal from the burn I received.

But it gave me good burning "food for thought."

Isn't sin just like this?

First, we break away from our Guide to go explore and see what we can find/do on our own.

Next, we get pulled by something that promises to be a rich, creamy satisfaction to feed our desire.

Then we find ourselves just "having a taste." "It won't hurt me." "I can control this."

And before we know it, we get burned. We are surprised that such a small taste can cause us so much pain.

If only I would've stayed the course with the tour guide, I would have been shown the truth about what was really in those trays that held the lye.

"For this, God is our God for ever and ever;
He will be our guide even to the end" (Ps 48:14).

The Core of Desire

"Delight yourself in the Lord and He will
give you the desires of your heart" (Ps. 37:4).

Have you ever been stuck in the thought, what do I *really* want? Have you mostly let the world define the answer? "Oh, she seems so happy because she has..." "If only I could live like that..."

I wonder what it would look like if each of us chased after our core desires. What if we could go to the true source and discover what drives us to our desires?

I was seeking answers to this very question while doing a study called "Walking with God." I spent some time asking God to reveal my heart's desire in light of the verse above. I was pleasantly surprised by his answer.

I love creativity. I was seeking the right avenue to express it, so I asked God to direct my heart to the things that would fulfill that desire. I expected him to expose when, where, and how to use my creativity. That was just me limiting God and putting him in a box. I think I forgot that I was asking the Creator of creativity!

Instead, what I heard him say to me through his Word and Spirit was this: "I want you to believe that you are valuable to me."

Two things struck me about this.

First, God went to the *core* of my desire. He is keenly aware that I need to feel valuable.

Secondly, He gives us the freedom to *choose* how to use our gifts. He just wants us to remain in him and the truth that he is at the core of our desires.

I love that he knows me better than I know myself, better than the world can define me. I don't think it's a coincidence that it was right after God created the world for five days that he said on the sixth day, "Let us make mankind in our image, in our likeness." (Gen. 1:26).

However we express ourselves, it is rooted in the Creator. What an honor to be able to reflect him at our very core.

The Jail and the Bird

Life has a way of startling us sometimes.

A robin accidentally got itself trapped in our garage, and no amount of flapping into the window was producing freedom. I opened up the window, but the bird kept trying to escape through the glass. I opened the garage door thinking it might need a bigger space. That didn't work either. It wasn't until I gently nudged the bird toward the open door that it found its way to freedom.

I felt bad for the bird. I know that she was nesting and all she could see out that window was the tree where her babies were and she just wanted to get to them. I could tell she was scared, but more than that, she was determined to get to them.

It touched me deeply because I could really relate.

A few days before this happened, I received a phone call that someone very dear to my heart had been arrested and was sitting in a Los Angeles jail. His choices finally caught up to him. There wasn't a day that I didn't think about him in that jail cell. Everything in me wanted to "fly" to him and make sure that he was in a safe place, but that's not what he needed.

He needs the key to freedom. I'm not talking about a jail cell key. He would eventually walk out those jail doors but would still be a prisoner. He needs Jesus. He needs a savior who can unlock the prison cell of his heart and set him free.

I ache over this because, just like that robin, I have shown the way to freedom in Christ but he has chosen to stay trapped and crash into the windows of life. I long for him to escape those trappings and find real freedom.

So I wait. I wait on Jesus to open the right window at the right time.

"It is for *freedom* that Christ has set us free" (Gal. 5:1).

The Last Straw

There are so many lessons that God teaches us when we rub shoulders with the homeless. A team from our church was serving in the kitchen of a shelter when several homeless folks came for lunch. I chose this as my first serving location, and after meeting the "people of the street," I asked if I could stay working there for the rest of the week.

My heart became enlarged for these people. It's one thing to hear about the homeless and feel compassion. It's quite a different experience when you have a face-to-face encounter and hear their stories. On the second day of serving lunch, a young woman came in and took a seat at one of the many tables. She had a certain ailment that caused her to struggle with body fluids coming from her mouth and nose. As I approached her to give her utensils, she looked up at me and I saw the emptiness in her eyes. Her life had been hard. I wondered if she had ever been invited to a fancy table for a feast or if she had always dined in homeless shelters.

I wondered if it bothered me because *I* knew what it was like to dine in a fancy place or even to sit in the warmth of my home with a grand meal before me. Was it even something that was on her radar? Did she only know this life? Did she find joy in anything?

As I set her utensils before her, I accidentally gave her two straws. She looked down at the table, picked up both straws, and with the excitement of a child at Christmas, said, "I have two straws! I get two straws!"

I was so humbled. I thought of the many, many times I had stopped for fast food, got an extra straw, and just pitched it in the garbage. It had no value or purpose to me. She, on the other hand, saw it as a gift!

And I was ashamed. I had become cold and calloused to the neediness that is in *all* of us. It caused me to wonder how many times I had "tossed" aside a person because they had no value or purpose for my life.

We *all* have been lost sheep. We *all* have value. We *all* matter to Jesus.

I love the illustration of the lost sheep in the Bible. In Matthew 18:12–14, Jesus says, "What do you think? If a man has a hundred sheep and one of them goes astray, will he not leave the ninety-nine on the hills and go out to search for the one that is lost? And if he finds it, truly I tell you, he rejoices more over that one sheep than over the ninety-nine that did not go astray. In the same way, your Father in heaven is not willing that any of these little ones should perish."

Each of us has been nothing more than dust, like that simple, meaningless straw. But Jesus looked at us and, like that young woman, saw in each of us that we are *all* a gift worth saving!

The Okay People

I picked up my eight-year-old granddaughter from school. The ride home was filled with an interesting discussion about heaven. Chloie wondered if heaven was filled with lots of old people. She wondered if you are old when you die, do you stay old.

We talked about the Bible telling us there will be no more pain or tears (so I guess that eliminates all the aching old people!). I shared how we will be getting new bodies that will never grow old.

We talked about how we get to heaven…that Jesus provides the way as our Savior.

We talked about how there is a real heaven and a real hell.

Then she asked this question.

"Nina, is there a place for Okay People?" I asked what she meant by Okay People.

She said, "People who are good people but have done some bad things too."

I told her, "That would be all of us, Chloie. But getting into heaven isn't because we are good or bad. It's because Jesus was perfect and took the punishment of our sin on the Cross. If we trust in him, that's how we know we are going to heaven."

Then she sighed. "I can't wait to go to heaven. But I kind of want to see what my life is going to be like here for a while."

Me too, precious girl. Me too.

Live your life well. Live your life for Jesus.

The Hallmark of Love

There once was a commercial for Hallmark where a woman was reading a card and you could hear her reaction resound throughout the store. Whatever she was reading, it caused her to burst out laughing. Sometimes cards just do that. They hit you right where you are.

I have spent hours over my lifetime looking for just the right card with the right message. I love giving and receiving cards, so I have no issue with this industry. It's a wonderful creative outlet for many artists.

I have a hope chest full of cards given to me, each telling me something that was worthy enough for me to keep. And many of those were given to me on Valentine's Day, the day of celebrating love…because the calendar says so.

But there is just something about receiving a message of love that is *required* that leaves it a bit…well, empty. We have all heard the saying, "Love is a choice." We've all heard and longed for unconditional love. Maybe you have never experienced this kind of love.

Can I send you a "Valentine" message right now?

God's love is unmatchable, uncontainable, undeserved, unearned, and eternal!

Romans 8:38–39 says, "For I am convinced that neither death nor life, neither angels nor demons, neither the present nor the future, nor any powers, neither height nor depth, or anything else in all creation, will be able to separate us from the *love* of *God* that is in Christ Jesus our Lord."

Just read that again! Have you ever received love, only to have it taken away from you? Jesus is not an Indian giver. Have you ever felt unworthy of the love you receive? Jesus can't wait to shower you with his. Have you ever thought you had to do something to receive love? Jesus wants you to receive just because he has so much love to give. He must give it away.

Receive it! And receive this promise: "May your unfailing love be my comfort" (Ps. 119:76)

Jesus is the lover of your soul. Not because Hallmark commands it, but because heaven commands it.

Best Valentine's Day card ever.

The Nosebleed Seats

We have all heard this term used when talking about being at the highest point of stadium seating. No one wants these seats. No one thinks they are prime seats. However, having the highest point of view can have its benefits.

In 1999, our eldest son graduated from high school. We were thrilled! Not because it was graduation day, not because it was a milestone in his life, but because we were holding our breath wondering if he would make it. School and studying were just not his strong suits. But by the skin of his teeth, he graduated.

It was what happened after the caps were tossed high into the air that was the most thrilling moment of the entire ceremony.

Picture with me the main floor covered in a sea of bodies, families trying to find *their* graduate. I made my way into the crowd searching for my son. Watching from high above was my good friend Anita. Later, she shared this story with me.

She said, "I wish you could have seen what I could see from above. As you were making your way through the maze of caps and gowns trying to find Chris, he was desperately searching for you, knocking over chairs to get to you. He would look up at me and lip the words, 'Where is she? I can't find her.' It was so obvious that he was on a mission to find you. Friends were trying to stop him along the way, but he remained fixed on his goal to reach you." She said, "Watching him find you and embrace you brought tears to my eyes."

As I reflected on this later, I thought about God's Son, Jesus, on his mission to find us. I wonder how God felt watching his only Son knock over more than chairs to reach us? How did he feel watching his Son remove every obstacle to embrace us with his love?

God is the ultimate Pursuer. He stepped into flesh so he could pursue us. He would not be detoured by friend or foe. His eye was on the prize, you and me.

I remember the first time I wept while reading Scripture. The reality of what Christ gave up and endured just hit me so clearly.

Read Philippians 2:5–8, "In your relationships with one another, have the same mindset as Christ Jesus: Who, being in very nature God, did not consider equality with God something to be used to his own advantage; rather, he made himself nothing by taking the very nature of a servant, being made in human likeness. And being found in appearance as a man, he humbled himself by becoming obedient to death—even death on a cross!"

Couple this verse with John 1:1–3, In the beginning was the Word and the Word was with God, and the Word was God. He was with God in the beginning. Through him all things were made; without him nothing was made that has been made."

For the longest time, I thought Jesus began his life when he was conceived by the Virgin Mary. As my understanding grew, I came to realize that he always was, always is, and always will be. He was enjoying his unmarred reign in the heavens as part of the Trinity long before his head was laid on a bed of straw in Bethlehem.

He gave up *so much* to reach us. He was surrounded by the heavenly praises of the angels, enjoying uninterrupted fellowship with God the Father and God the Holy Spirit. And although he remained God the Son while he fulfilled his ministry on earth, he was forever marked by his Crucifixion. He endured all the pain and suffering that came with stepping into a dark and fallen world.

And the entire time he was on the Cross, each of us was on his mind.

"He made himself nothing."

The King of kings and Lord of lords did not use his true position to his advantage but gave it all up to reach us. And he endured not only death, but the kind of death that was reserved for the worst of criminals.

Why did I weep so when I read Philippians?

Reality hit.

His humility replaced my lowly status with a royal standing.
His sacrifice took his life and gave me mine.

And I have heard someone once say, "He would have done this if you were the only person on the face of the earth."

Just let that sink in.

The Pain-Taker

I ventured to her home again. She didn't want me there, really, but my love for her wouldn't keep me away. It's not easy to walk into a room so oppressed with the tensions of anxiety and depression, especially when the person of your focus is someone you have adored since birth.

My sister. My baby sister.

I cautiously made my way to her side, this person who is normally full of life and laughter, a quick-witted person who always made us smile. But here tonight, she was inwardly drawn, melted into her couch, hoping she could disappear along with her painful, debilitating struggle.

But it doesn't. It burrows into the very core of her, winning the battle of her will, convincing her that she has no hope.

Words don't come easy. What can I say that hasn't already been said? What can I do that hasn't already been done? My mind races for answers, but I come up empty-handed. I sense her wanting to leave, to check out, to let the world go on without her…but I can't really bear that thought.

So I sit silent, stroking her hand just so she can feel the tenderness of another's touch, so she will know she matters, that I see her in her pain and despair. I want her to know that she is not alone.

My mind begins to wander. What would I do to make her pain go away? What extent would I go to release her from her despair? I have often heard people say to another who is suffering, "I wish I could take your pain" or "I would give anything for this to be me and not you."

And that's when it hit me. My love is shallow compared to the love of Christ.

Internally, I asked myself, "Would you take Joan's pain and despair for your own if it meant Joan would be free from it?" And I took one look at her and I knew in that instant that the answer, the honest answer, would be no.

It would have been easy to begin self-loathing. Instead, it made me fully and keenly aware of two things:

One, I don't love as deeply as I think I do.

Two, I am overwhelmed that, when faced with the same decision, Jesus didn't even bat an eye to say that he would do this for me. He just did it in the ultimate extreme.

And my heart swelled. I love that Jesus saw my pain and suffering, my living under the curse of a fallen world, my sin and rebellion, and said, "I am going to take care of this. I am going to take it on myself and set you free."

That is the love I know.

The Rock

Michigan is known as the Great Lakes State. We are surrounded by five lakes, each with its own unique characteristics. It wasn't until my good friends moved to the Upper Peninsula that I stepped foot on the shores of Lake Superior.

As women who love to craft, my friend Tammy and I decided to try our hand at rock painting. Her husband Steve took us to Lake Superior to look for the perfect rocks. After we walked over a swaying bridge, rock bags in hand, ready to collect what we could find, I barely stepped into the sand when I spotted my first perfectly-shaped rock. I was so excited that it could be that easy to find what I needed. As I bent down to pick up the rock, I heard Steve laugh under his breath. I figured he was reacting to a silly girl getting so excited about a rock! He said, "C'mon."

He led me to where his wife Tammy had already headed, over a sandy hill, which was only feet away from my big find, and it all became clear. Laid out before me as far as the eye could see was miles and miles of rocks in all shapes, colors, and sizes. I dropped the rock that was still in my hand and just said, "Oh wow!" I looked at Steve and he was grinning. He knew what was to come when we walked over that hill. He knew that one rock in my hand would pale in comparison to what would be spread out before me as a rock feast! He knew I had limited sight and just needed to take a few more steps to find the jackpot.

Jesus did the same thing with his disciples. In Matthew, he began to prepare them for his departure. Peter wanted to know why he couldn't follow Jesus where he was going. He had become their rock and they wanted to scoop him up and keep him for themselves. They couldn't imagine life being any better if they let go of him.

Jesus told them, "Do not let your hearts be troubled. You believe in God; believe also in me. My Father's house has many rooms; if that were not so, would I have told you that I am going there to prepare a place for you? And if I go and prepare a place for you, I will come back and take you to be with me that you also may be where I am."

He reminded them that he *is* the Rock, but they had to let him go so he could reveal that he was the Rock for all the ages. He couldn't be the Savior if they kept him tucked away in their own proverbial rock bags. He had to expand their vision for the masses.

I imagine a few of them had their own "oh wow" moment. Like Steve, who had already been to the shores of Lake Superior and knew what was waiting for me, Jesus had already walked the shores of heaven and knew what was waiting for his disciples, then and now.

So the next time you are holding fast to something, believing it's the answer, and Jesus says, "C'mon," just go. Head to where he leads. I guarantee that he will lead you to a much more satisfying experience.

The Prisoner

If you read the words "she/he is a prisoner," what would that conjure up in your mind? You might think of a man sitting in a jail cell waiting to be released or you might think of a woman in an abusive relationship and has no way to escape. Being a prisoner doesn't invoke very uplifting thoughts.

But listen to this. In Zechariah 9:12, God is speaking to his people, telling them to return to their fortress and calls them "prisoners of hope." He knows that people get disheartened because our vision is so limited, but he sees from a whole different perspective. If we could see what he sees, our despair would be turned to hope. He gives us snippets of his goodness so our hope will remain intact.

I have never thought about being a prisoner of hope. What an interesting twist. Let's unpack that thought.

If you had nothing else but hope, it would have similarities to being in prison.

- It would be all you have.
- It would keep you from relying on anything or anyone else.
- It would surround you and consume you no matter what direction you turn to.
- It would drive you to a new purpose, a new outlook.

Hope is the key to unlocking us from living in the many false prisons that we allow.

Praise be to the God and Father of our Lord Jesus Christ! In his great mercy, he has given us new birth into a *living hope* through the resurrection of Jesus Christ from the dead and into an inheritance that can never perish, spoil, or fade (1 Pet. 1:3–4).

The Window Pain

No, that is not a misspelling. And even though a window "pane" is meant to be looked through, I wondered if this was the experience of a gentleman who traveled on the same train as me.

As my husband and I took our first train ride to Toronto, I was fascinated by the people all around me. There was a group of senior citizens passionately engaged in friendship and laughter. There was a pleasant young woman traveling solo. People were all going to "something."

And then there was an elderly man sitting directly across from us, alone, except for the cane resting near him. He wore simple clothing and a scowl that deterred anyone from approaching his personal space. He spent most of the trip gazing out the window as the landscape flew by.

I wonder, though, what did he *really* see as he looked out that window? I wonder if that window became a backdrop for memories of his life to play out before his eyes.

What flashed before him? Loss of loved ones? Loss of health? What made him scowl at the young woman who asked if the seat next to him was taken? What made him use his cane as a barrier between himself and people? He was as cold as the windowpane he gazed out.

The contrast between this man and the group of seniors behind him was staggering. It was a clear picture of engagement with life vs. engagement with loneliness.

In Proverbs 18:14, it says, "The human spirit can endure in sickness, but a crushed spirit who can bear?"

I believe we daily walk (or ride) among the crushed in spirit. I wish I could relive that moment of traveling with that lonely stranger. Even if he never spoke a word to me, I would have loved to fill up the space next to him and kick out the lies that may have played out in his head, telling him he was alone and that there was no one who cared about him. His cane would've been an easy barrier to break. His spirit was not. This was a good life lesson for me. I hope this is also a good lesson for all of us, to keep our eyes, ears, and heart open for the lonely and marginalized. I don't think there is a person on this planet that wouldn't benefit from knowing that they matter.

The Wicked Witch in All of Us

One of my favorite classics is *The Wizard of Oz*. I've watched it since I was a child and the magic never goes away. As an adult, I've wondered what the draw was for me. It could be so many things: a journey out of the mundane black and white into a colorful adventure, the dedicated friendship of the characters she meets along the way, or the reality that home wasn't such a bad place. I can't get through the scene when she is back home and says the words "There's no place like home" without welling up with tears.

I think what most strikes me is Dorothy's journey of courage. She battles her way through all that the Wicked Witch throws at her until she reaches Oz and the promise of returning home. She keeps her eye on the prize.

Shortly after I became a Christ follower, I had this idea to rewrite *The Wizard of Oz* with an evangelistic theme. After all, it has so many parallels to the Christian faith. When it got to the point of casting the characters, I decided to play the Wicked Witch. I imagine that some would think that that would be a difficult role to play. I even had someone say to me, "How are you going to do that role? You're too pretty and too nice."

Funny, but I actually thought, of all the characters, this one would be the *easiest* to play. If I'm honest, being "wicked" is closer to my inner reality, my fallen, sinful nature. Deep within each of us is a natural bent wicked witch. We battle against what is good, right, and true. We grow green with envy when someone has something we don't have: financial freedom, a more loving husband, children who love the Lord.

It's quite humbling what bubbles up out of us.

And the impact we make on one another when we operate from our sinful nature can have lasting effects. There were children who wouldn't come anywhere near me after I played that role. They couldn't separate that the Wicked Witch and me were two different people. They literally would back away from me.

I think Paul knew what this felt like. After his conversion, many didn't trust him. They still saw him as a wicked man, killer of Christians. There was no trust.

> "When he (Paul) came to Jerusalem, he tried to join the disciples, but they were all afraid of him, not believing that he really was a disciple" (Acts 9:26).

Who in your life has had a reputation for being unloving but has been transformed by the power of Jesus Christ, and yet you are holding them to their "old self"? Aren't we *all* battling against the old self? I imagine a different world where we see one another the way Jesus sees us.

> "You were taught, with regard to your former way of life, to put off your old self, which is being corrupted by its deceitful desires; to be made new in the attitude of your minds; and to put on the new self, created to be like God in true righteousness and holiness" (Eph. 4:22–24).

It's ironic to me that Dorothy used water to melt the Wicked Witch, removing her as an obstacle so she could journey on.

Jesus does so much better. He baptizes us into the Holy Spirit so we can journey well.

And if we think the Emerald City was beautiful, just wait until we get a look at our future heavenly city. I think I will be crying again and saying, "There's no place like home."

The Weeping Song

To stand or to fall
It matters not to me,
For to stand is to be lifted up
By the very promises of God.
And to fall is to taste the sweet grace
He first extended.

To weep or to sing
It matters not to me.
For to weep is to sense home
And long to see his face before me.
And to sing is to be home and have
His gaze upon me.

To sit or to dance
It matters not to me,
For to sit at his feet
And hear his gentle voice
Or to dance on the streets
Made of pure gold.

To live or to die
It matters not to me,
For to live is to gain
To die is to be with
My Savior of all eternity.

Watching from the Shoreline

I love that the Word of God is alive. It always amazes me how I can read a passage that I've read many times before and see something new illuminated. It's like God takes a flashlight and shines it right on the specific words he wants to reveal in his timing.

That happened as I read Mark 6:47–48: "*Later that night*, the boat was in the middle of the lake and he (Jesus) was alone on land. He saw the disciples straining at the oars because the wind was against them. *Shortly before dawn*, he went out to them."

The disciples were in trouble. Jesus saw they were in trouble late at night, but he didn't respond until shortly before dawn! What was he doing? Sitting on the shoreline shaking his head? Having a late-night snack? Why didn't he go to them immediately?

I think the answer is in verse 52: "For they had not understood about the loaves; their *hearts were hardened*."

I believe that Jesus often sees and is aware of our struggles or our need for him, but he delays interceding to teach us something. Sometimes, he delays to awaken something in us that would otherwise remain the same.

In *My Utmost for His Highest*, Oswald Chambers wrote, "If I can stay in the middle of the turmoil calm and unperplexed, that *is* the end of the purpose of God… God's end is to enable me to see that he can walk on the chaos of my life now."

I pray that each of us can be just as mesmerized when Jesus sits on the shoreline waiting for the perfect time to reveal himself as we are when he gets up and walks on water toward us. He was still there, just one wave away. And he is still here now, just one prayer away.

What the Heck Are You Talking About?

Have you ever found yourself asking this question when God asks you to do something that makes no sense? Have you ever read his word and thought, "I'm sure he didn't really mean *that*." I think this is more common among believers than we realize. After all, Jesus was a pretty radical man. And the Scripture does say, "Who can understand the mind of God?"

Even the disciples, who lived intimately with Jesus, asked this question.

Imagine sitting around with a man you are hoping is the Savior of the world with a plan that will knock the socks off of the oppressive governing leaders. You take a sip of your wine and dip your bread, and as you do, Jesus opens his mouth and says, "We are going up to Jerusalem and everything that is written by the prophets about the Son of Man will be fulfilled. He will be delivered over to the Gentiles. They will mock him, insult him, and spit on him. They will flog him and kill him. On the third day, he will rise again."

Oh, by the way, sweet dreams tonight.

Can you imagine the pillow talk conversations that night?

Luke 18:34 says, "The disciples did not understand any of this. It's meaning was hidden from them and they did not know what he was talking about."

Can you hear their confusion?

"What the heck is Jesus talking about? He's the Savior!"

"Is he crazy?"

"I'm just trying to figure out what he really meant."

"Maybe we need to go back and read what the prophets wrote. I must've missed something."

"*Is* he crazy?"

"I'm not sure this is what I signed up for."

I want to cut the disciples some slack. After all, this conversation happened preresurrection. I'm sure there was a lot that made no sense to them.

But it begs the question, why do we still ask the same questions when we are post-resurrection? Everything the Prophets and Jesus predicted came true. Not one prophecy has been wrong.

My prayer for each of us is that the Lord would increase our faith. I pray that we would search His Word and walk away with nothing but praise for what he has already done and a new excitement for all that he is still going to do.

Two Fathers Collide

Have you ever been in a really dark place and feel stuck? I found myself here during a recent bout with anxiety. Each day became more and more of a struggle just to get out of bed and face the day. On one particular day, I felt such an oppression in my home and it was so tangible that I knew I needed to go to battle against the enemy. As I cried out to the Lord for deliverance, his soft whisper said, "Leave your home and go where you know the Holy Spirit is alive and thriving." Immediately, I knew where I had to go. I had recently become connected with a new ministry in the area called Barn45. There was a walking path through the woods all the way around this barn. That's where I knew I needed to head. I had never once stepped on this property during the summer and not felt the tangible presence of the Holy Spirit.

As I began trekking on the path, I began crying out to the Lord for his presence and his help. I felt desperate for a touch from his healing hand. I had my phone with me and was listening to a song I loved, letting it seep into my mind. The song was reminding me that I am loved when I don't feel like I am, that I am strong even when I feel like I've got nothing left.

I walked circle after circle around Barn45 listening to that song on repeat, tears spilling down my face. After circling the path about three times, my phone rang. I looked to see who it was, and instantly my heart fell. It was my dad calling. You would have to know my dad to know that this was the last person I wanted to talk to in this moment. But something told me to answer the phone. I took a deep breath and tried to compose myself before saying hello.

All he said was, "How you doin', girl?" And I lost it. The tears began all over again. I told him the truth. "I'm not doing well, dad. I'm really struggling."

I expected his usual response to kick in. Try to "fix" me, make a joke or two to try and avoid my pain, and talk about stuff that didn't really matter to me. But he didn't do any of these this time. Instead, with a tenderness of voice, he said, "Well, I have two ears. I can listen."

You have to understand that this response from my dad was so foreign to me, but it did the trick. I opened up and shared, and he listened. Before I knew it, I was having a stroll and conversation with my dad.

After we hung up, I looked at my phone and said out loud to the Lord, "What the heck was that all about?" And as clearly as if the Lord was strolling along with me, I heard him whisper, "I didn't want you to believe you were walking alone, so I sent you your earthly dad to 'walk with you' to remind you that your Heavenly Father is right here walking with you. You are not alone."

My Heavenly Father knew that I needed my earthly father as a reminder of what fathers are meant to do. They are meant to care for, provide, and fight for their daughters. I was beginning to wonder if my Heavenly Father had forgotten about me, but he took a few moments out of his holiness to speak directly into my loneliness. And he did it with the least likely person I would suspect that he would use.

I smile as I write this because there are two words written inside Barn45 on one of the wall studs. As it was being built, Joy, the cofounder of Barn45, asked all the women at the summer Bible study to write their favorite Bible verse on the studs of the barn as a marking that would be permanent before the drywall went up. I couldn't make it the night they did this, but I asked her to inscribe the words "Never Alone" for me. She did and sent me a pic. I keep it as the background on my tablet to remind me daily of this truth.

Thinking we are alone and *being* alone are as vastly different as our earthly father is to our Heavenly Father.

Paul reminds us in 2 Corinthians 10:5b: "We take captive every thought to make it obedient to Christ."

Every thought…

When the enemy says, "You are so alone," Jesus says, "I'm right here and I'm not going anywhere."

When the enemy says, "You are defeated," Jesus says, "I have made you more than a conqueror."

When the enemy says, "You have much to fear," Jesus says, "Don't fear, for I have redeemed you; I have called you by name; you are mine!" (Isa. 43:1).

Can I challenge you with this experiment for just one day? Pay really close attention to the thoughts that are getting cemented in your head. See how often they turn to fear, anxiety, and lies. Then seek truth and replace each thought with one truth from the God who is alive in you.

> "For though we live in the world, we do not wage war as the world does. The weapons we fight with are not the weapons of the world. On the contrary, they have divine power to demolish strongholds" (2 Cor. 10:3–4).

When Did You Know He Was the One?

Many speeches have been made at wedding receptions that tell the story of when a bride knew that "he was the one." I've heard this declaration whether the couple had been together five months or five years. The amount of time together doesn't always seem to determine how well these newlyweds truly know each other.

I wondered this as I read Matthew 8:23–29.

Jesus had begun his earthly ministry. He had called his disciples. They were living up close and personal with him. I wonder what they had experienced. Amazement? Doubt? Excitement? Concern? Did they ever wish they hadn't answered the call to "Come and see"? I wonder what it would have been like to strap on my sandals and follow him every day.

Certainly, by the time we read this story, they have seen the authenticity of Jesus and have heard him make claims about who he is. I am surprised by their question in verse 27 after Jesus calms the wind and waves of a storm. It says the men (disciples) were amazed and asked, "What kind of man is this? Even the winds and waves obey him!"

I am not surprised that they were amazed at the power he displayed. That *would* be pretty amazing to see. What I am amazed by is that they wondered what kind of *man* did this. Did they really miss who he claimed to be? Before I come down too hard on the disciples, I need to turn this question to me and you. How often have we seen the miraculous power of Jesus Christ and then doubt him when we face the trials of life? I don't know about you, but I can sure have short-term memory when it comes to believing Jesus for his promises.

The story goes on with a second detail that amazes me. After Jesus calms the storm, their boat arrives on the other side in the region of Gadarenes. He no more than touched his sandals to land when he was approached by two demon-possessed men coming from some tombs. The Bible says they were very violent men and no one could pass that way. We aren't told what they would do to make it impossible to pass, but they reveal something about their awareness.

Remember the question the disciples asked about who Jesus was as a man? Well, these crazy, violent, demon-possessed men *answer* the question!

"What do you want with us, *Son of God*?" They knew who he really was! And they knew his power. They were so afraid that they begged him to cast them out into a herd of pigs! And even in this request, Jesus displayed his power...again. Was it for the sake of the disciples? I wonder what they were thinking and feeling as they watched this showdown of power between good and evil. Did it boost their confidence in the Son of God?

Is the life of the disciple today any different? Is my confidence and belief in the Son of God so rock-solid that no crisis will bring me to a breaking point of doubt in who he says he is? My prayer for each of us is that Jesus would disrupt our world in ways that would stretch our awe of him.

Let's fall so in love with Jesus that people who know us begin to ask, "When did you know that he was the One?"

When How Becomes Why

One of the most impactful passages in the Bible to me is Philippians 2:6–8. I have actually wept over this passage when the reality of what Jesus sacrificed hits me at my core.

> "Who, being in very nature God, did not consider equality with God
> Something to be used to his own advantage;
> Rather, he made himself nothing by taking the very nature of a servant,
> Being made in human likeness.
> And being found in appearance as a man, he humbled himself by becoming obedient to death—
> Even death on a cross!"

How is it even possible that the God-man, the second person of the Trinity, the Savior of the world, "did not consider equality with God something to be grasped"?

How is it even possible that the King of kings and Lord of lords would "make himself nothing, taking on the very nature of a servant, being made in human likeness, found in appearance as a man"?

How is it even possible that the Captain of all the angel armies, the God-man who has all power at his very fingertips, would "humble himself, becoming obedient to death—even death on a cross"?

Now, go back and change the first word of those three questions that start with "how" and change it to the word "Why."

A little three-letter word...*how*...changed to a little three-letter word...*why*...equals a little three-letter word...*you*.

While he was on the cross, *you* were on his mind.

I was on his mind.

He gave up Trinity status, trading celestial air and the highest ranking in the heavens, marking his unblemished body with a permanent scar for all eternity, because of *you*. Because of me.

He took care of the how. I am humbled by the why.

There is no greater love.

And he continues to take care of the hows in our life.

And here's the really cool part.

God established Jesus' position because of his obedience.

> "Therefore God exalted Him to the highest place and gave him the name that is above every name." (Phil. 2:9).

And we are called to live in the same obedience.

> "That at the name of Jesus every knee should bow, in heaven and on earth and under the earth, and every tongue acknowledge that Jesus Christ is Lord, to the glory of God the Father" (Phil. 2:10–11).

When Humor Is Better than Fear

My husband has a great sense of humor. It's one of the character traits that drew me to him. It's infectious and can override just about any situation. Even in moments of fear, it has steadied me. I guess our sons picked up on that.

I had a pretty big scare when I was told that I might have MS (multiple sclerosis). I didn't know how my sons would take the news. I was hoping that they wouldn't be filled with fear, as I was, so I tried to downplay it and also remind them that we have a big God who would take care of us. I was certain that the news would destroy them.

So you can imagine my surprise when I heard about this conversation between them after they were both told.

Chris (to Bryan): Have you talked to Dad?
Bryan: Yeah. (And then he filled Chris in on my testing.)
Chris: Does Mom have a good will?
Bryan: I don't know, but I know I'd get her Dickens Christmas village.
Chris: I just want the fake Christmas tree.
Bryan: Well, the doctors are giving her four months.
Chris: Could they bump it up to two months so I can get the Christmas tree?

Best. Medicine. Ever.

When things seem scary and out of control, just remember who had the last laugh at the Cross.

"Oh death, where is your victory? Oh death, where is your sting?" (1 Cor. 15:55).

Jesus dealt with the worst news ever, the fallen sinful nature of man, but he went to the Cross and trusted the Father for restoration so that he could laugh in the face of death. So can we.

What Snorkeling Taught Me about Life

Have you ever noticed how many times in life we go through the motions, unprepared and uncertain, letting the unknown paralyze us and keep us from experiencing the greater plan that God has for us? I certainly have lived many moments like this. I've often wondered what I've missed from living in fear, denial, lack of knowledge, or trust.

It kind of reminds me of the time I went snorkeling for the first time. I had no idea what to expect, but the instructors knew exactly what I needed to have the most fulfilling experience.

The first thing you need is the right equipment. You need an air tube, flipper fins, and goggles. As in life, God provides us with all the right equipment to enjoy life to its fullest. His Word is as necessary as the air we breathe, he equips us with the proper armor (see Eph. 6:10–17), and he gives us new eyes to see.

The second thing you have to do to snorkel is get in the water. You can have all the right equipment, but if you stay on the boat and don't get in the water, your experience will be nonexistent, dry. It's the same with entering into life with God. We have to step into the battles, the callings, the opportunities.

Third, you have to get horizontal. You cannot properly snorkel unless you lie down in the water. The same is true for our relationship with God. To experience him fully, we often need to lie face down before our Creator in humility as "he who began a good work in you is faithful to complete it."

Fourthly, you have to let go of your fears. I'm not sure why, but as I slipped into the water, I began to hyperventilate. Maybe it was the thought of breathing through an air tube or maybe it was the fear of the unknown, not knowing what was in the water around me. But for whatever reason, I had to let go of my fears before I could put my face below the water's surface. If I had stayed stuck in my fear, I would have missed all the beauty that was waiting for me. The same is true in our relationship with God. If we only focus on the surface of our circumstances, we will miss out on the depth of joy and beauty that God has for us.

God is interested in the heart. The Bible says, "The purpose of a person's heart are deep waters, but one who has insight draws them out" (Prov. 20:5).

Fifthly, you have to be aware of the dangers. Once I put my face into the water, I was inundated with a world of beauty. The fish and coral reefs were so colorful and stunning. However, our instructor had prewarned us that we were not to touch the coral because it could cut you and/or the coral could die. Sometimes, when we let God into the deep waters of our hearts, it can feel like he is cutting us to the core as he reveals the unlovely things about our character. But the good news is, he tenderly reveals for the purpose of bringing beauty out of his revelations. God has been giving us fair warning since the days of Adam and Eve. He warned them not to touch the tree of knowledge of good and evil or surely they would die. We have been flirting with sin ever since. If we ignore God's warnings about the dangers of sin, we can be cut or die spiritually, emotionally, and even physically.

Lastly, once I put my face in the water, I saw things in God's creation that I didn't even know existed. It was like stepping into a whole new world and this is what God offers us. He says, "I want you to see the beauty of my creation, including yourself, with a whole new perception. I want you to see people as I see them. I want you to see circumstances as I see them. But you have to ask me for a new perception."

I love that God sees us so vastly different than the world sees us. 1 Samuel 16:7 says, "The Lord does not look at the things man looks at. Man looks at the outward appearance, but the Lord looks at the heart."

> You are loved.
> You are treasured.
> You are sought after.
> You are found.

When Focal Points Mock Us

When I became pregnant with my first child, I was one of those new moms who was going to do everything that was best for her and her child. And since it was the days when getting an epidural was a no-no, I prided myself on being counted as one of the strong ones who would endure natural childbirth.

My husband and I went to a Lamaze class to learn all the techniques that promised, if done correctly, would make childbearing a breeze. Breathe like this, sit like that, and most importantly, make sure you have a focal point. Choose a picture or some object that you can place in your view and when the contractions come, focus on this object.

I chose a picture of some random cute baby from a magazine. I figured it would remind me that, at the end of all the pain, I would be rewarded with an adorable little being. I posted it at the end of my hospital bed. When the contractions were mild to moderate, I locked eyes with that little face. I drew strength from those piercing blue eyes.

However, when the contractions became intense, all I could focus on was the pain. My focal point was no longer a face cheering me on but a source of mockery! It no longer held promise of the good that was to come on the other side of my pain.

I lost my focus!

And don't we often live life the same way?

As a believer in Jesus Christ, I have an eternal focal point. I have the promise of the Holy Spirit living in me. I become a member of the kingdom of God and the promise of a home with no more pain and no more tears. But sometimes I live like his promise is no more real than that piece of paper during my labor. I get caught up in the "laboring of life," the pain, and disappointments, and I lose my focus.

Jesus said, "A woman giving birth to a child has pain because her time has come; but when her baby is born she forgets the anguish because of her joy that a child is born into the world. So with you: *Now is your time of grief*, but I will see you again and you will rejoice, and no one will take away your joy" (John 16:22).

Jesus reminds us that we will have grief in this life, but keep our eyes on the focal point…we *will* see him again and we *will* rejoice. So push! Push through the pain!

When Life Grabs You by Surprise

Modesty is a trait my mother taught me. I'm not one of those people who would comfortably get undressed in front of other people, like my girlfriends or strangers. I just like my privacy!

My friend Tammy and I decided to check out a small-town tearoom and do some shopping beforehand. We spotted this little boutique and wandered inside. I was in the market for a bathing suit and some lingerie.

The owner and her daughter immediately approached us. I told her what I was looking for and she became my personal assistant. Beyond my personal assistant. She invaded my personal space.

As I entered the *only* changing room, complete with a curtain for privacy, I began the process of trying on items. My friend Tammy was right outside the curtain. Without warning, the woman stepped into the already tight space of the changing room and decided that I was clueless about how to properly try on a bra. The minute she stepped in, I felt completely exposed. She reached around me to "assist" certain parts of my body getting into a bra the proper way! I stood there like a deer caught in the headlights! What just happened? And standing behind her was my friend watching the whole thing go down.

As quickly as I could, I got dressed and exited the boutique. My friend looked at me and I at her, and I said, "What the heck just happened?" We kept shaking our heads and trying to process before we burst out laughing. We laughed all the way back to the car. We were still processing on our drive home when we both realized that we completely forgot to go check out the tearoom! And we started laughing all over again.

As I reflect back on that moment, I think about all the different ways that we can have our plans and intentions laid out before us and then something comes along and "grabs us by surprise." We wonder, why did that happen to me? Why are we being allowed to suffer? Why didn't God intervene? Why? Why? Why?

What is interesting to me is the fact that we have actually been warned ahead of time. None of our trials are a surprise to the Living God.

Read what 1 Peter 4:12 says: "Dear friends, do not be surprised at the fiery ordeal that has come on you to test you, as though something strange were happening to you."

We should *expect* life to grab us by surprise.

But what are we to do when it happens? Many of us go into shock, like I did in that store. Many of us flee and get as far away from the situation as we can. Yep, me also. But the Word goes on to say this about trials: "But rejoice inasmuch as you participate in the sufferings of Christ, so that you may be overjoyed when his glory is revealed."

My story is a silly, humorous experience. Most of us face things that can be hard and debilitating, especially when we didn't see it coming. But the Lord reveals that *nothing* is wasted to bring glory to his name. Nothing we go through in this life is separate from his knowledge and plan.

Read 1 Peter 4:13 again. We are not suffering alone. We are participating in the sufferings of Christ. And in doing so, he stays right beside us so that we may be overjoyed when his glory is revealed.

Stay committed. Keep faith. Keep hope. For we have the *privilege* of sharing in his suffering *and* in his glory.

When Our Eyes Shift

One summer, my family went to Mackinac Island and stayed at the Grand Hotel. They have a beautiful ballroom, so we decided to go listen to the full orchestra playing. As we sat at our table, a very young girl and her father stepped onto the dance floor. She would stand on her daddy's shoes as he swayed her back and forth, dancing. The whole time, she was looking up at his face as if to ask, "Do you think I'm special, Daddy?" I was so mesmerized by their moment. Maybe it stirred a longing. I don't know, but I couldn't stop entering into their private moment and soaking it in.

However, my concentration was soon broken. All eyes shifted to a very beautiful woman stepping on the dance floor, dressed to kill, voluptuous, and screaming "Notice me" in her body-fitting red dress. And she could dance.

The little girl and father faded into the background.

Later, I reflected how quickly I was distracted from the innocence of that little girl and her father. Their dance was touching a longing in me to be embraced and cherished by a father, like she was. But I let the longing be overshadowed.

Is this how God feels about us when he says, "You have forsaken the love you had at first" in Revelation 2:4? What causes us to so quickly forget that we are a bride-to-be in waiting?

Let's take a walk to an imaginary park, sit on a bench, and listen in on an intimate conversation.

Woman: "You are the treasure that I have sought for so long. You are my all in all. You're all I want. You're all I've ever needed."

Overflowing with excitement, the divine lover proclaims the passion of his heart.

"How I love you! You are priceless and precious beyond words. I ache for you to know my heart. I made you to be loved and to love freely in return. Oh, how I love these moments when, hand in hand, we share the thrilling oneness of intimate hearts."

Woman: "Look, there's an oak tree over there. Let's go carve our names in it to show the world our love."
Divine Lover: "I will do much more than that to proclaim my love for you, my beloved. It's not good enough to carve your name next to mine on a tree that will one day wither away. Instead, I'm going to carve your name on the very palm of my hand."

And then the proposal comes and he asks her to be his alone, his bride! And she says yes!

And the divine lover says, "All I ask of you is that you love me with pure devotion."

The days go on. The engaged woman and her divine lover connect in deep, soulful ways, until one day she becomes distracted by other things in the park. It no longer fulfills her to just sit on a park bench basking in this immense love. So she doesn't show up to their bench one day, but she does show up in the park. She comes down the boardwalk strutting her stuff and vying for the attention of another. And she engages with one "adulterous lover" after another. And there, on the bench, sits her true love, watching, weeping, and longing for her to return to him. Day after day, he watches as she flirts with another, thinking it will fill her and touch her on a soul level.

And he waits. And he saves that spot on their bench for her alone.

And when she returns, with mascara streaking down her face and her heart broken, she says, "I thought it was what I needed."

And he painfully says, "I know."

And we say, "It felt right at the time."

And he says, "I know."

And we say, "I am so sorry."

And he tenderly draws us into his arms and says "I know," realizing he will have this conversation over and over and over again as we return to our adulterous lovers.

Yet, he makes a passionate plea: "Don't you realize there is no one who can love you like I do? And I will wait for you as long as it takes. I've loved you from the first moment I laid eyes on you. My very soul is anchored to yours."

The search for what we *think* we want is usually not what we really need.

I was reminded of this while watching the movie *Sense and Sensibility*. One of the characters, Marianne, is seeking a spirited love with someone who cherishes her deeply. We are introduced to two characters: Colonel Brandon and Willoughby.

Colonel Brandon loves and cherishes Marianne but won't force his love on her. He feels like he would go mad if he couldn't be with Marianne and love her for the rest of his life. He is very representative of how Jesus is as our bridegroom. Then there is Willoughby, who is wild and free-spirited. Marianne is drawn to him (false lover?), but he eventually chooses wealth and status over her, leaving her with a broken heart.

And aren't we like this today? Always searching for someone who will cherish us deeply and often settling for the "Willoughbys" that leave us brokenhearted? And all along, Jesus (like Colonel Brandon) just longs to be with us and love us for the rest of our eternal lives.

May I ask a question? What or who are the "Willoughbys" in your life? What or who have you put in place of your affection for Jesus? It could be a person that you are demanding meets your needs, a hidden or obvious sin that you run to as a numbing agent. We have a choice where to place our affections. And so does our bridegroom.

And here's the amazing thing. He leaves the door open and walks toward us even when we have been unfaithful. Whenever we truly confess our sin and take steps back to him, he welcomes us with open arms.

"I have loved you with an everlasting love"
(Jer. 31:3).

When Your Wish Is Granted

Everyone knows that you can't ask a genie to grant you three more wishes as one of your wishes. It is apparently cheating. And it cheapens the three wishes that have to be really thought out, so you make them count.

The word grant means to agree to give or allow. Businesses grant maternity leave for pregnant mothers. College students seek grants for their schooling. By all measures, being granted something is a good thing.

So, when we come to the passage in Philippians 1:29, we might think that this is a grant gone sideways.

"For it has been *granted* to you on behalf of Christ not only to believe in him, but also to suffer for him."

Say what? We are granted suffering? I didn't ask for that. I'm just interested in the happily ever after of eternal life in Jesus Christ. I signed up for the saving, not the suffering.

Just like asking for three more wishes, accepting the pass into the pearly gates and rejecting our participation in his sufferings is also cheating. They go hand in hand.

> "Dear friends, do not be surprised at the fiery ordeal that has come on you to test you, as though something strange were happening to you. But rejoice inasmuch as you participate in the sufferings of Christ, *so that* you may be overjoyed when his glory is revealed" (1 Pet. 4:12).

If we're all honest, I think each of us sees God as a genie at one time or another. Someone rubs us wrong, so we rub the God-genie bottle. A prayer goes unanswered, or at least it seems that way to us, so we reiterate our request, just in case God didn't hear us the first time.

In the movie *Aladdin*, he asks genie what he would wish for if he had a wish. He says, "Freedom." Aladdin is surprised by that. He looks into the opening of the genie bottle and says, "You're a prisoner?" Genie says, "It's all part of the gig. Phenomenal cosmic power, itty-bitty living space," and crawls back into his lamp to prove his point.

I wonder if God ever feels this way since giving us freedom to choose. He has phenomenal cosmic power, beyond anything we could ever imagine, but does he ever feel limited by our freedom to choose? He will not force us to love him or follow him. He often allows the wickedness of our fallen world to appear in control, yet in that he allows us "freedom." We can choose to be sprung from our itty-bitty lives into the freedom of Christ. Yes, his suffering as well as his glory, but freedom nonetheless.

When Our Whys Are Rewritten

Looking at the lives of the disciples is not a warm, fuzzy experience. Jesus allowed every one of them to face pain and suffering. And he left each of them with a "why" on their lips.

One of the biggest roadblocks to relationship with God the Father or God the Son is the questions that start with why.

Why would he allow that?

Why wouldn't he intercede in that circumstance?

Why would he send his only son to a senseless and cruel death on the Cross?

Why would he slaughter people in the Old Testament?

Why would I ever follow such a cruel God?

We all have our whys.

Every road we travel is paved with whys. Every crossroad has a billboard asking why.

And here's the funny thing about the English language. We have a vocabulary full of words that sound the same, but a different spelling of it can completely change the meaning.

What if our *why* thoughts were turned into *wise* thoughts? What if our whys and doubts were given over completely to the all-wise God, the God of all wisdom and knowledge?

How different would our lives and perspectives be? How different would we live if we knew that nothing surprised God, nothing happens that he doesn't already have plans to use.

Whether you're traveling on a very long road that seems to have no end or you are standing at a crossroad, God has already taken that road trip. He sees where you are going and he is ready to take the trip with you.

"For I know the plans I have for you," declares the Lord, "plans to prosper you and not to harm you, plans to give you hope and a future" (Jer. 29:11).

"To the *only* wise God be glory forever through Jesus Christ" (Rom. 16:27).

Pack your bags (not your baggage). It's time for a road trip!

Where Am I Pinning My Interests?

A few years ago, a phenomenon hit the web that has either been a blessing or a curse to many. Pinterest (which got its name from the concept to "pin" your "interest") has become a go-to site for many a crafter, cook, photographer, bride, home decorator, etc.

I know women who gauge so much of their decision-making against the ideas of Pinterest. I've heard jokes from women who say their husbands are going to divorce them if they spend one more minute on the site. I know women who say they will not even go to the site anymore because it "became an addiction."

I am a Pinterest user. One of the things I like to use it for is quotes. When I do a newborn photo shoot, I often like to add a quote to bring some emotion to the image. I stumbled across this saying, which has since become a very popular one for pregnant moms.

"I am in love with a child I haven't met yet." It speaks of the bond that happens with mothers as their unborn child grows within them.

Peter, an apostle of Jesus, shared thoughts that are completely parallel to the experience of carrying a child. Let's look at a few verses from 1 Peter 1:3, 1:6, and 1:8.

> "In his great mercy he had given us 'new birth' into a living hope…"
>
> "Though now for a little while you may have had to suffer…"
>
> "Though you have not seen him, you love him." Sound familiar?

Our relationship with God is so similar to the journey of carrying a child.

- There is a time when we don't physically see each other.
- There is a unique beginning, a choice, to birth these relationships.
- There is an awareness of "life" growing inside of us.
- There is a longing to meet face-to-face.
- There is pain/discomfort in the process of this life growing in us/spilling out of us.
- There is an incredible bond when you look face-to-face into unconditional love.

I can still remember clearly the moment I looked into the face of each of my sons for the first time. My emotions were all over the place. I can only imagine it pales in comparison to the first glance of being face-to-face with Jesus. Let Jesus be your addiction. Spend as much time with him as you can. Live your life and choices around him. Pin your interests on the Savior. Your life will never be the same.

When Snakes Take Up Residence

I am not a fan of snakes. I am especially not a fan of snakes when they get into my house! When my family moved into our first house, I bubbled over with excitement at the thought of decorating and making this "home"! Because it was a small house, we decided to finish the basement and make it our family room. We completed it with a drop ceiling, a fireplace, and carpet to keep warmth all around us.

One night, as we were watching TV, we heard a noise that was unfamiliar. It sounded like someone was above us shuffling along in their slippers. It would stop and then start again. As we silenced the TV, we listened intently to narrow down where the noise was coming from. Just as it began again, movement caught my eye at the corner of one of the light covers in the drop ceiling. *Snake*! There was a snake in our drop ceiling.

What transpired next was nothing short of adrenaline-driven comedy. You see, I grew up with a brother who had garter snakes as pets. I even took one to school for show-and-tell once. So when I saw this little guy slither across that light panel, it was startling but not frightening. Not so much for my husband. He is deathly afraid of snakes. He went into hyper mode, driven by a deep fear of what he was about to face.

After putting on the thickest gloves he could find, grabbing a golf club and a net, he was geared up to take down his greatest fear. As he pulled down the soft ceiling panel on an angle, we were given full view of the snake. It spanned the entire four feet of the panel! That little garter snake just became a full-grown giant beast to be slayed!

Sometimes, looking at the motives in our heart can look exactly like this.

Often, we don't get a clear picture of what's really going on underneath the surface. We only see the insignificant "tail end" of the bigger picture. We pretend that the problem isn't really that big.

It can be scary, but when we peel back the layers of our heart, we get a better picture of the problem and it's usually not pretty. We are face-to-face with the bigger problem, just like that snake when the ceiling tile was pulled back.

Once we reveal what's truly under the surface, we have choices. We still had the problem of how to deal with the snake. I suppose we could have kept it, given it a nice name, and made it our pet. Not likely, but don't we do that with sin? We embrace it, give it a nice name, and make it our own.

Or we could have pushed that ceiling tile back in place and pretended the snake wasn't there. But we all know that wouldn't take care of the problem. Often in heart matters, we come up with some game plan to change our external behavior so no one can see what's really going on underneath the surface.

My hubby decided to take down that pesky snake and beat him to death, leaving behind a stain and stench. Trust me, if you've ever smelled a reptile house at the zoo, you know it's not a pleasant smell.

The only other option we had available to us was to invite someone else to come and take care of the problem, but we are creatures who often act autonomously.

In matters of the heart, we have someone who can and will reveal the true nature of our hearts.

Psalm 51:10 says, "Create in me a clean heart, O God *and* renew a steadfast spirit within me."

God, who knows the depths of our heart, tells us that a clean heart is something that can only happen in relationship with him. And a clean heart is something that needs constant attention and renewal.

Jeremiah 17:9 says, "The heart is deceitful above all things and beyond cure. Who can understand it?"

Psalm 139 says, "O Lord, you have examined my heart and know everything about me… Search me, O God, and know my heart; test me and know my anxious thoughts. See if there is any offensive way in me and lead me in the way everlasting."

The way I see it, he has an impeccable record of dealing with snakes from the beginning of time. Who better to give my heart problem to?

Who Do You Belong To?

When I was pregnant with my second child, my four-year-old crawled into bed with me one morning and, for the first time without my nudging, he asked if he could feel the baby in my tummy. It was a sweet moment of bonding and confirmation that he was going to be okay giving up his title "baby of the family."

I told him that we were going to the hospital that day to take a tour. He put his mouth up close to my tummy and said, "We're going to the hospital today to see where you're going to sleep, baby, but you will be in the same room right next to Mommy so you won't be scared or lonely." I said, "The baby will be in a nursery with all the other new babies." He looked at me with great concern and said, "Then we won't know which baby is ours!"

As I recall this memory, I am reading from Isaiah 43 and I had to laugh at the imagery that God speaks to the nation Israel. He says, "Do not fear, for I have redeemed you; I have called you by name; you are mine. When you *pass through the waters*, I will be with you…"

How do I explain to a four-year-old that even before my water breaks and this child passes from the womb to the world, I will *know* he is mine? I will be able to go to the nursery, and with certainty, I will redeem *my* child. Why? Because I will be the first to hold him. He will bear the image of his father and me, and I will burn his features into my memory. I will call him by his new name and I will claim him as mine. I will begin the journey of walking alongside that child all the days of his life.

It's interesting how many times the Lord says, "Do not be afraid" in the book of Isaiah. And he always qualifies it with "I will be with you." Sometimes, don't you just feel like a four-year-old with God?

"But I'm afraid!"
"I will be with you," says the Lord.

"But how will I know if this is right?"
"I will be with you."

"I can't do this alone!"
"I will be with you."

Never. Ever. Alone.

Your Eyes

I've waited for this day most of my life
It's my personal day of reckoning
I stand before you, Jesus
Finally, here we are, face-to-face

Your eyes, they seek me out
And penetrate my soul
Your holy gaze upon me
I stand before you whole.

Jesus, it's only because of you
I stand before you now,
Your pure and holy bride
With joy I take this vow.

My eyes are filled with tears
To see you face-to-face
It's all because of you,
It's all because of grace.

No eye has ever seen
No ear has ever heard
No mind could ever comprehend
The meeting of my Lord.

My heart can hardly take it in
To know he ransomed me from sin
He alone deserves my heart,
Oh Holy One, set apart

LAURIE POWERS

What is this now upon your face?
Tears flow freely, tears of grace
To think your love is now complete
I fall and worship at your feet.

Look at me in paradise
Sought out by my Savior's eyes
The Bridegroom searched and found his own
No words describe this welcome home.

The Waiting

Dreamlike…
Bright, inviting light…

Anticipation…
Glimpses of…what is before me?

The scent of celestial air, fragrant…
An aroma that fills my senses
One minute the sweetness of oranges,
The next, the fragrance of pungent roses.

My eyes, they are closed.
I focus only on the sweet scent.
Lemons, cinnamon, the smell of fresh dew.

And now my barefoot walk is tantalized by the
Soft carpet beneath my feet…sand? Plush grass?
It feels like silk beneath my toes.
A cushy softness I've never felt before.

My eyes perk alive to the sounds of water…
Waves upon a shore? The tumbling of a waterfall?

Aah, the serenade of the birds singing songs I've never heard.
So angelic.
Perhaps it is?
Is that the song of angelic beings in the distance?

The anticipation gains momentum, and I open my eyes with no fear of disappointment.

Oh, my brother Paul, who had a small glimpse of heaven, had it right when he said that the Lord has prepared for us beyond what we could ever imagine. "No eye has seen, no ear has heard, no mind can conceive what he has prepared for us" (1 Cor. 2:9).

My eyes can hardly take in the paradise before me. It appeals to every one of my senses. Never had I seen such beauty, smelled such aromas, tasted such sweetness in the air, or heard such blissful melodies. And this is just at the entrance of the new heavens and new earth!

I delight inside the depths of my soul because it dawns on me that I haven't even set eyes on my Savior yet...or even more so, that he, my Jesus, the pure Lover of my soul, has not yet set *his* eyes on me.

And now all fades to the background as I see him approach, his eyes locked on me, his pure, spotless bride. I stifle a giggle, the joy so uncontainable. His eyes pierce my soul with intense passion. His walk becomes a quick gait, moving closer to me with open arms. I know it is he, for I see the remaining scars of his sacrifice.

I can bear the weight of this intense joy no longer and I fall to my knees before my Jesus. He forbids it, taking his place before me, reaching gently to me, lifting my face to his, and that's when I see it.

A never-ending love in his eyes. Unspoken words—yet all that I've longed to hear is spoken in that one moment of eternity.

My Lover...me...finally face-to-face, *never* to be separated again.

And as he warmly embraces me, I hear him whisper, "Welcome home."

About the Author

Laurie Powers has been journaling for over forty-five years using some of her life stories to speak at women's retreats and youth retreats, through drama and into the hearts of women. Laurie bravely followed a calling to debut her personal writings in this book, believing that her story, intersected with God's story, would continue to encourage. Laurie has been married for thirty-five years to Tom, whom she affectionately calls "hubby." She is a mother of two sons and is blessed with seven grandchildren. In her free time, Laurie loves photography, creating scrapbooks for her grandchildren, and spending each morning alone with Jesus.

CPSIA information can be obtained
at www.ICGtesting.com
Printed in the USA
BVHW071456141019
561050BV00003B/198/P

9 781098 002480